the **SOUND ON SOUND** book of

home recording

made easy

professional recordings on a demo budget

Design: David Houghton

Printed by: Black Bear Press Limited

Published by: Sanctuary Publishing Limited, The Colonnades, 82
Bishops Bridge Road, London W2 6BB

ISBN: 1-86074-199-1

the **SOUND ON SOUND** book of

home recording

made easy

professional recordings on a demo budget

paul white

contents

CHAPTER 4

CHAPTER 5

CHAPTER 6

CHAPTER 7

CHAPTER 8

introduction

Home multitrack recording has revolutionised music by enabling anyone with musical ideas to record and mix their own compositions without the need to hire expensive studios. The other major revolutions in music making are MIDI and sequencing, which provide the musician with access to a vast range of sounds, both realistic and abstract. The technology that makes all this possible is now affordable enough for almost anyone to get involved with, yet the quality of the end result can rival or even exceed what was possible in top studios just a couple of decades ago. Used properly, even the simplest home recording set-up can produce unbelievably good results, but as with all technology, you have to understand how to use it properly if you're to get the best out of it.

Traditionally, home recording has involved recording onto tape, but now we have the choice of analogue or digital tape, and tapeless recording onto computer disk. However, the majority of the computer-based systems aim to emulate, as closely as possible, an analogue tape-based environment, so the majority of this book describes the traditional tape-based method of working, though digital tape and tapeless systems are discussed in some detail. Once you're familiar with the traditional processes involved in recording, you'll find they translate quite easily to the more modern tapeless platforms.

The purpose of this book is to help you make the most of home recording by taking you through the whole recording and mixing process. You don't have to be particularly technical to use recording equipment any more than you need to know all about photography to use an automatic camera, but as with all practical subjects, there are right ways and wrong ways to do things, as well as useful shortcuts to be learned. The author has had many years' experience in recording and has stripped away much of the jargon and mystique that surrounds the subject to explain the whole recording and mixing process in a straightforward, non-technical way.

You can only fully master recording by actually doing it, which is why this book takes a very practical approach, comprehensively illustrated with easy-to-follow diagrams. No matter whether you are working with a simple cassette deck and two mics, or a full multitrack recording studio, this book will help you produce more professional results. More than two decades of experience are concentrated in these pages, making *Home Recording Made Easy* one of the most useful studio accessories you'll ever own.

chapter 2

basic concepts

While the aim of this book is to make recording your own music as 'hands-on' and non-technical as possible, there are certain operational principles that must be understood in order to operate recording and mixing equipment effectively. I've tried to keep this chapter as simple as possible, but please take the time to read it at least once before progressing to the rest of the book.

While it is possible to record music onto analogue tape, digital tape, hard disk or removable magnetic and magneto optical computer media, analogue cassette-based systems are still the easiest to understand, and the majority of tapeless systems make a deliberate attempt to emulate a traditional 'tape' way of working so as to place the user in as familiar a working environment as possible. To explain the underlying process of multitrack recording, I have made a conscious decision to stick with the old 'analogue tape' model such as is used in cassette multitrackers, but digital alternatives will be covered in a later chapter.

The main point of multitrack recording is that it enables recorded compositions to be built up one part at a time rather than everything having to be played, mixed and recorded in one go. This makes it particularly attractive to the solo musician working at home, who may want to play many or all of the musical parts himself.

A conventional analogue tape machine, such as a cassette deck, employs a 'record head' which converts the incoming music waveform into an alternating magnetic field. This field is what transfers the magnetic information from the head onto the magnetic tape. When the tape is played back, the magnetic message now stored on the tape is read by a playback head, then amplified to reproduce the original electrical signal. The exact physics is of course a little more complicated than that, but it isn't necessary to know precisely how a tape machine works before you can use it anymore than you need to know how a telephone works to call your friends on one.

tape tracks

Magnetic tape is really just a flexible strip made from a durable, non-magnetic material, coated with a layer of specially formulated oxide partiles that are able to retain magnetic information. The simplest form of recorder is the single-track or mono machine, which writes the magnetic information as a single, invisible stripe along the length of the tape.

Because tape is designed to be reusable, an erase head is positioned just in front of the record head so that when you make a recording, the erase head wipes the tape just before it arrives at the record head. If you think of the magnetic recording as being the magnetic equivalent of pictures drawn in sand, the erase head effectively shakes the sand until it's level again by applying a high frequency magnetic field to the tape. Another way of looking at it is that the erase process randomises the magnetic information on the tape, effectively removing any recognisable signal that may once have been stored there.

Stereo recorders actually make two different recordings side by side along the tape in the form of two parallel tracks. One track feeds the left loudspeaker of a stereo system and the other feeds the right hand speaker. A stereo record head is really just two heads in one – one to record the left hand signal and one to record the right. Similarly, the playback head is also two heads in one.

cassette tapes

With a Compact Cassette, you turn it over once it's got to the end which lets you record more music 'on the other side'. This isn't actually recorded on the other side of the tape (the terminology is a throwback to vinyl records which did have two sides), but rather the two recordings are on the same side, running in the opposite direction. If you could see the individual tracks, you'd see something like a two-lane motorway with side one being represented by two lanes running in one direction and side two by the two lanes running in the other. This is made clearer by the diagram in Figure 2.1 which shows how the tracks are recorded on a stereo Compact Cassette.

The figure also shows how the tracks are arranged in a 4-track multitrack recorder. Note that the track layout is the same, except they are now all recorded in the same direction and are all played back at the same time. This means that you can't turn the tape over – it's only used in one direction. It's also important to understand that there is no difference between a mono, a stereo or a multitrack tape cassette. Recording tape is

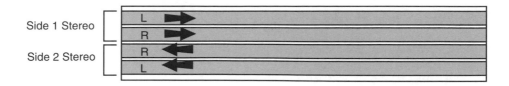

Figure 2.1a: Track layout on a stereo cassette

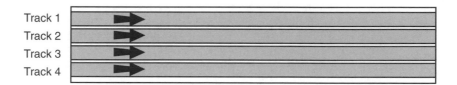

Figure 2.1b: Track layout on a multitracker

a single strip of flexible plastic coated on one side with magnetic material. The tracks themselves are created by the record head in the tape machine.

multitrack recorders

Multitrack works on the same principle as stereo, but instead of being able to record only two tracks at once (right and left), you can record, four, eight, 16 or even more tracks depending on the choice of machine. Eight tracks is the current maximum for cassette-based systems. These tracks may be recorded all at once, a few at once or all independently depending on how you want to work. You could either record a live performance, then mix it afterwards, or build up your composition an instrument at a time. In practice, most people record the first few tracks all at once, then add extra instruments and vocals afterwards in a process known as overdubbing – the main point is that you can work whichever way you feel most comfortable.

Being able to build up a recording in layers offers several advantages – one musician can play or sing many different parts in the same piece of music, and when the recording is finished, the levels of the different tracks can be balanced and panned to give the perfect mix. Even when all the musicians play together, multitrack provides the ability to record each instrument and voice separately, allowing the relative balance and tone of the various instruments to be adjusted during mixing.

overdubbing

After the first tracks have been recorded, you need some way of hearing these play back while you overdub new parts. For example, if your band has just played the bass, drums and rhythm guitar part to a song, you need to hear this while singing the lead vocal or playing the guitar solo. Listening to a signal being played back on a tape machine is known as monitoring, and when recording overdubs, this is generally done using headphones to prevent the previously recorded sound spilling back into the microphone.

tape monitoring

On early multitrack machines, different heads were used for recording and playback, and this led to timing problems when overdubbing because the record head was several centimetres further along the tape than the replay head resulting in a fraction of a second delay between the recorded and replayed sound. Complicated switching systems were devised to get around the problem, but all cassette multitrackers and virtually all modern semi-pro open-reel multitrack recorders use the same head for both recording and playback which neatly avoids the problem. Figure 2.2 shows the delay problem associated with older multitracks and also the simpler modern system using a combined play/record head.

A single tape track can be used to record only a mono signal, so stereo signals need to be recorded onto two tracks which must then be panned right and left in the mix to recreate the original stereo image. In many instances, signals are recorded in mono and then positioned across the soundstage during the mix using pan controls. For example, there's little point in recording a lead vocal in stereo. Though there are some advantages to recording some instruments in true stereo, the limited number of tracks available from a cassette multitracker makes stereo recording something of a luxury.

punch-in punch-out

The concept of multitracking basically involves recording different tracks at different times and then mixing these tracks to stereo so the result can be recorded onto a conventional stereo tape machine. However, few people make flawless recordings, so before you can mix, you need some way to fix any mistakes or wrong notes you may have recorded. The process by which small parts of a recording are replaced with new sections is known as punching in.

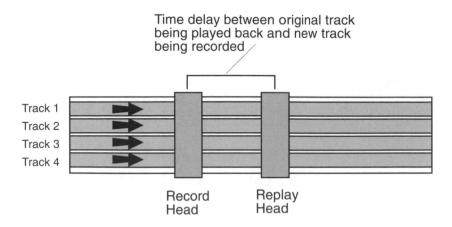

Time delay between original track
being played back and new track
being recorded

Track 1
Track 2
Track 3
Track 4

Record
Head

Replay
Head

Figure 2.2a: Separate record and replay heads

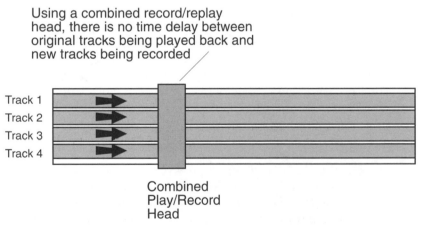

Using a combined record/replay
head, there is no time delay between
original tracks being played back and
new tracks being recorded

Track 1
Track 2
Track 3
Track 4

Combined
Play/Record
Head

Figure 2.2b: Combined record and playback head

Imagine you've recorded a vocal part on track 1, but one word turns out to be sung flat. You don't have to sing the whole song again – you simply start the tape a few seconds before the mistake, sing along with what's already recorded and then, at the right moment, put the machine into record (just on the vocal track!) without stopping the tape. At the end of the new section, ideally between words or phrases, you punch out of record again and you have your repair.

Punching in is very simple but you need to punch in and out during a slight pause, otherwise the repair won't necessarily be seamless. Why? There's always an overlap in the old and new recorded material at punch-in due to the physical distance between the erase head and the record head. When you punch in, the erase head will turn on, but the short section of tape between the two heads still contains previously recorded material because it passed the erase head before it came on. Consequently, as new material is recorded, it will overlap the old material by the time it takes the tape to move from the erase head to the record head.

When you punch out, there will be a slight gap as the short section of tape between the erase head and the record head will already have been erased and nothing new recorded onto it. This might only last a quarter of a second or so, but if it happens in the middle of a sound rather than during a pause, you'll almost certainly be able to hear it.

So, how do you do a punch in? Many multitrack machines allow you to punch in by first setting the track (or tracks) in question into 'record ready' mode using the individual track Record Ready buttons. The punch-in is then executed by putting the machine in to play, then holding down the Play button while pushing down the Record button at the punch-in point. You can punch out again by hitting Stop or, sometimes, by hitting Play. Another system is to put the machine into record with no tracks selected as 'ready', then use the Record Ready buttons themselves to drop in and out. Some recorders also let you use a footswitch for punching in which is perfect for musicians working on their own. Consult your multitrack manual to find out how your machine handles punching in and out.

auto monitoring

Before the drop in, the existing recording is monitored, preferably via headphones which means you can sing or play along to get the feel of the piece. When you punch in to record, the monitoring automatically changes from playing what was originally on the track to the new part that you're recording, and when you punch out of record again, the monitoring goes back to playing the recording from tape. Any tracks not set to record will continue to play normally during a punch-in.

Because most tape machines can handle the monitor switching automatically when you punch in or out, you always hear the right thing in your headphones which means you get to concentrate on your performance, not on technicalities.

When recording pop music, it sometimes helps to make the punch-in and punch-out points coincide with a drum beat so as to hide any slight discontinuity which might occur at the edit points. Even if you find suitable gaps to punch in and out, you might find the sustain of the instrument is still audible at the edit points, and without a beat to disguise it, there's a chance you might hear the edit. Similarly, it's important to start playing before the punch-in point because the act of punching in may record over the sustain of a note that was playing beforehand. By playing the same notes as the original part before the punch-in point, any sustained notes will be duplicated making the edit less obvious.

bouncing

At first, having four or even eight tracks to record on seems wonderful, but very soon, you'll find you want to record more parts than you have tracks. The way around this is called 'bouncing' – the process of mixing together two or more already recorded tracks and re-recording the result onto a spare track. If you're working with 4-track, the most you can do in one go is to record three tracks, then bounce them onto the fourth which leaves the first three tracks free to be used for new recordings. This process is shown in Figure 2.3. All home recording equipment uses the same tape head for recording and playback, so the bounced recording is always in perfect sync with the original tracks. It is very important to check the quality of a bounced mix, because once you've wiped over the original tracks, there's no going back.

If you need to really stretch the capacity of your recorder, most multitrack machines will allow you to add one part live as you're bouncing, so you

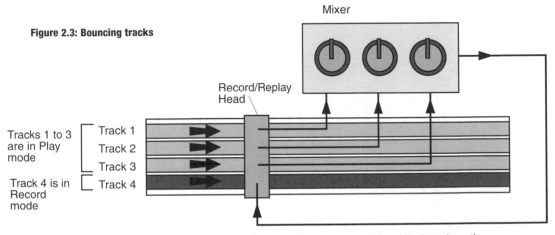

Figure 2.3: Bouncing tracks

Mixer

Record/Replay Head

Tracks 1 to 3 are in Play mode

Track 1
Track 2
Track 3

Track 4 is in Record mode

Track 4

Tracks 1, 2 & 3 are combined in the mixer, then recorded back onto track 4. This is known as 'track bouncing'. After bouncing, tracks 1, 2 & 3 are free for reuse could, for example, play a synth part live while bouncing your drum machine, rhythm guitar and bass parts onto a single track giving you a total of four parts on one track. Those working with other musicians can also record two or more parts at once on the same track – but you won't be able to change the balance of these two parts afterwards.

10-track bounce

Using a 4-track machine and adding one 'live' part every time you bounce means a solo musician can get ten different parts onto tape without ever having bounced any sound more than once. The so-called 10-track bounce works like this:

★ Record tracks 1, 2 and 3.

★ Bounce tracks 1, 2 and 3 to track 4 while adding a new 'live' part. If you make a mistake recording the live part, you'll have to go back to the start. You can't punch in successfully while working this way, so choose an easy part.

★ Check that track 4 sounds exactly the way you want it to – you're about to 'burn your bridges behind you'.

★ Record new parts over tracks 1 and 2, then bounce these to track 3, again adding another new 'live' part.

★ Again, check the result.

★ Record over track 1 and bounce to track 2 while adding another 'live' part.

★ Check the result.

★ Finally, record your last part back over track 1. Now you're ready to mix.

limitations of bouncing

When you bounce two or more tracks together, you are actually making a copy of your original recording onto a new tape track, and every time you copy a recording, you lose a little quality. The noise level increases and the overall clarity tends to suffer too. Even with a good machine, if you bounce more than once, expect to notice a drop in sound quality. The best quality will be maintained if you record at the optimum level and you should always use the meters on the recorder to help you get it right. I'll be talking a lot more about levels later in the book as poor level matching is responsible for most of the sound quality problems in home recording.

Using a standard 4-track machine, you don't have enough tracks to bounce everything in stereo so what you tend to end up with is four separate mono 'submixes' on the four tracks which you have to pan in the final mix the best way you can. A little forward planning can go a long way in making the best of this limitation and a useful tip is to try to keep all your bass and rhythm sounds together so you can pan them to the centre of the mix. Solos, sound effects and backing vocals can then be panned to other places in the mix to create the illusion of a wide stereo recording. Stereo effects help enormously here as we'll find out later.

what to bounce?

It's a fact that some sounds take more kindly to being bounced than others, and it's also true that a sound that will eventually end up right in the background can usually be bounced without compromising the final product. By contrast, bouncing a lead part destined to be high in the mix will expose any weaknesses. Bright or percussive sounds tend to suffer the most from bouncing so try not to bounce your drums or lead vocal parts if at all possible.

Once you've gained a little experience with your machine, you'll probably get familiar with the way sounds change when bounced, and you may be able to compensate to some extent by adding a little high EQ as you bounce to make up for the drop in brightness that bouncing invariably entails.

recording levels

I mentioned earlier that recording levels are vitally important; if you record at too low a level, your recording will be noisier (more hiss) than it should be, whereas if you record at too high a level, the sound will become distorted as the magnetic coating on the tape becomes 'saturated'. Check the meters on your tape machine when recording, then make a test recording to make sure that everything sounds okay. For most material, the level meters should go just a little way into the red on the loudest parts of your music but the absolute level varies from one machine to another and from one brand of tape to another. You'll also find that some types of sound show up distortion more than other. Vocals and overdrive-style electric guitar can generally be recorded fairly hot before you hear any distortion, while predominantly high frequency sounds like bells or cymbals, may distort well before the meters go into the red. For this reason, it's very important to make a few test recordings to see how your individual machine copes with different types of sound. Ultimately, all that matters is the sound, so listen first, then if the result is okay, make a note of the meter readings for future reference. I know that keeping a notebook isn't very trendy, but unless you have a perfect memory, it is the best way to keep a record of your settings.

trust the meters?

Short or peaky sounds, such as drums, often produce misleading meter readings on mechanical VU meters because the meter mechanism isn't fast enough to respond accurately to very short sounds. In fact a mechanical VU meter really shows you the average sound level as perceived by the human ear. With experience, you get used to what meter reading to expect with what type of sound, but most modern machines use bargraph meters which are less likely to be misinterpreted. Bargraph meters are faster and so more accurately represent the peak signal level, but you still need to run some tests to find the best levels. Of course your setting may change if you use a different brand of tape so it's best to find a brand you're happy with, then stick to it. Most cassette multitrack recorders are designed to use Type II or Chrome-type tape and it is false economy to use anything less than the best quality tape.

tape speed

You may have noticed that some cassette multitrack machines run at the same speed as a hi-fi cassette deck whereas others run at twice the speed. As a general rule, the faster the tape speed, the lower the tape noise and the better the high frequency response so you can expect better recordings from a double speed machine. The down side is that your recording time is cut in half. Because multitrack work only uses the tape in one direction, a C60 will last for 30 minutes at normal speed or 15 minutes at double speed. A good tip is to avoid recording anything on the first or last 15 seconds of the tape. If there's a problem with the tape winding evenly onto the hub, this is where it's most likely to cause sound quality problems.

varispeed

All modern multitrack recorders are fitted with a variable tape speed control known either as Varispeed or Pitch. The range is only a few per cent but it's enough to push the pitch of a recording up or down by more than a semitone which is very useful if you're trying to overdub a piano or other instrument that isn't in concert pitch. You simply use the Varispeed control to 'tune' your recording to the piano, record the piano part, then put the speed back to normal. Varispeed is also useful for helping out singers who can't quite make the high notes – you just slow down the tape a little and try again!

tape noise reduction

Semi-pro analogue tape recorders need to use some form of noise reduction system, because without it, the level of background tape hiss is likely to become obtrusive during passages where the recording isn't loud enough to mask it. Noise reduction systems provide an effective means of increasing the available dynamic range by reducing the subjective level of tape hiss during quiet passages.

To understand how systems such as Dolby work, it helps to know a little about what went before. There is a very old (but still valid) technique called pre-emphasis/de-emphasis, which entails applying a high frequency boost to signals during recording, then applying an equal degree of high frequency cut during playback. This restores the programme material to its original state, but the top cut reduces the level of any high frequency hiss caused by the tape itself.

Though simple pre- and de-emphasis is rarely used on its own to counter tape hiss, it illustrates very well that noise reduction comprises two stages – the encoding stage which is applied during recording, and the decoding stage where the exact opposite treatment is applied during playback. If the same noise reduction system isn't used both during recording and playback, the tonal and dynamic accuracy balance of the programme material will be compromised.

Tape machines are factory adjusted for a specific brand and type of tape, and using any other brand is likely to result in a level difference on playback that may upset your noise reduction system. If you want to use a type of tape not recommended for your machine, get the machine set up specifically for your choice of tape.

You don't have to know how noise reduction works so long as you appreciate that if you make a recording with noise reduction, you have to play it back using the same type of noise reduction. You also have to appreciate that such noise reduction systems only help reduce tape hiss – they don't have any effect on hiss that's recorded as part of your original signal. However, if you'd like to know a little more about the various noise reduction systems available, read the next section.

dbx

The majority of Tascam Portastudios, including the 488, use the dbx system which provides very high levels of noise reduction by combining HF pre-emphasis with 2:1 compression. If you don't know what compression is yet, check out the effects and processors section of this book. On replay, a 1:2 expansion (the opposite of compression), is used along with de-emphasis resulting in a maximum of 30dB of noise reduction. If noise reduction systems were judged solely on how much hiss they avoided, dbx would be an outright winner, but in reality, all noise reduction systems cause some side effects.

Using such a high degree of compression means that the replay signal from the tape machine must match the recorded signal very accurately, both in terms of level and frequency response. That's because the compressor/expander system magnifies level errors in such a way that a 2dB error in the tape machine becomes a 4dB error after decoding. In theory, this implies that the machines best able to benefit from dbx are those that are so good that they don't need it.

To get around this shortcoming, there are actually two different dbx formats; Type 1 for professional use and Type 2 for domestic sound equipment. Type 2 is used in cassette multitrack machines where the degree of noise reduction is traded off against a greater tolerance to machine and tape errors.

The way dbx works is to dramatically increase the level of quiet signals being recorded to tape with a view to overpowering the tape hiss with brute force. The expansion process on replay reverses the processing and returns the signal to normal, but it is sometimes possible still to hear hiss in the presence of low frequency sounds where there is no top end present to mask the hiss. A solo bass guitar or deep bass synth may be accompanied by noise which decays as the notes decay. There is little that can be done about this other than to optimise recording levels (and perhaps use some EQ when mixing), though in the context of a complete mix, it is rarely a problem providing recordings are made on good quality tape.

It's also important that when using dbx, the recording level should not be driven up into the red but should instead peak at around or just below 0VU. If you push more level onto tape, the tape saturation will cause audible decoding errors resulting in a dull or squashed sound. In any event, dbx is so effective in reducing noise that you don't need to push your tape to the limit.

dolby b

Dolby is still the best-known noise reduction system with Dolby B being the most popular version for use in domestic hi-fi cassette machines. Unlike dbx, Dolby B only comes into action when the signal falls below a certain threshold level where the signal is no longer loud enough to mask the noise.

Because hiss is most audible at higher frequencies, Dolby B treats high frequencies differently from low frequencies, and as such, it has a lot in common with pre-emphasis/de-emphasis. However, the frequency above which boost is applied during recording varies according to the spectral content of the programme material, and because high level signals that are loud enough to mask the tape noise aren't treated at all, there are fewer audible side effects. Only the vulnerable low level signals are subjected to HF boost. Dolby B is quite a well-behaved system but it can only achieve a modest 10dB of noise reduction.

It is essential that any recorder using Dolby B is lined up to give an accurate playback level, otherwise the decoding part of the system will come into action at the wrong threshold value. Dolby B is often accused of sounding dull on domestic hi-fi cassette decks, but I suspect this is largely due to poor machine alignment or a failure to both record and play back using Dolby B.

dolby c

Fostex use Dolby C noise reduction for the majority of their cassette multitrackers and open reel machines, though they have made Dolby B and Dolby S models too. Dolby C works in a similar way to Dolby B but includes anti-saturation circuitry to prevent HF tape saturation when top boost is being applied to already bright signals. By helping prevent tape saturation, decoding errors are reduced.

As well as being a more tolerant system than Dolby B, Dolby C provides up to 20dB of noise reduction. Playing a Dolby B encoded tape back via Dolby C will sound tonally incorrect but at least it's usually listenable.

dolby a

Dolby A has been around for almost three decades but is only ever used in professional recording machines. In recent years, Dolby SR has taken over as the preferred professional noise reduction system.

dolby sr

Dolby SR is Dolby's flagship noise reduction system and was introduced to give the analogue recorder a longer lease of life in the face of competition from digital machines. Up to 25dB of noise reduction is possible with minimal side effects, but Dolby SR is both technically complicated and very costly to buy. Dolby SR attempts to ensure that the maximum possible energy is recorded in all frequency bands at all times using ten filters, some with fixed frequency bands and others that vary to cover different parts of the spectrum dependent on the programme material. Anti-saturation circuits are included to prevent HF tape overload.

Dolby SR enables analogue recordings to sound cleaner and more transparent than the best digital recordings and it is reasonably tolerant of level errors and tape speed changes. Dolby SR is unlikely ever to find its way into semi-pro recording equipment, but the newer Dolby S system offers some of the benefits of SR without the high cost.

dolby s

Dolby S is strictly a semi-pro/consumer system but is related to Dolby SR, which is why SR was discussed first. Even so, it would be wrong to think of Dolby S as a low cost version of SR because in most respects, it's more similar to Dolby C, with some of the filter technology from SR added. Dolby S sounds more natural than either Dolby B or C, but although it is much cheaper than SR, it still costs significantly more than Dolby B and C.

If you don't fully understand the technicalities, at least you'll now know what noise reduction can do for you, and also that to benefit from it, the recording has to be both recorded and played back with the noise reduction switched on. Though all noise reductions introduce side effects of varying degrees, these are generally minor compared with the level of background hiss that would be present if noise reduction were not used.

notes on tape care

Quality recording starts with good quality tape, but unless that tape is stored carefully, it could start to deteriorate, putting your precious recordings at risk. Tape should be stored in a dust-free environment (a sealed plastic bag is fine), out of direct sunlight and at a steady room temperature. Because tape is a magnetic medium, it should also be kept well away from magnetic fields such as are generated by loudspeakers, VDUs' power supplies and so on.

Never leave tapes in the car or close to radiators as direct sunlight and heat can greatly shorten the life of recording tape. Avoid damp or dusty atmospheres, and always ensure the tape machine is clean, especially before making important recordings.

gain structure

On an artistic level, the concept of gain structure is pretty boring, but it is the key to making the best recordings of which your equipment is capable. Failure to pay attention to this vital subject will seriously compromise the quality of your recordings, and even professional equipment will perform extremely poorly if the rules explained here are not followed.

The human ear can hear sounds ranging in level from the dropping of a pin to nearby thunder – even the very best recording equipment fails to match the dynamic range of the human ear. In music, we never need to go to these extremes – our quietest sounds are rather louder than dropping pins, while the loudest sounds fall well short of the power of thunder. This leaves us with a more realistic dynamic range, which properly used electronic equipment can cope with, but even so, this still involves signal levels varying from just a few microvolts up to around 20 volts.

At the start of any audio chain is the microphone, and once the signal has left the microphone, it is electronically amplified to bring it up to line level, then passed through a complex chain of circuitry which may include mixers, equalisers, amplifiers, effects units and routing systems being recorded onto the master tape.

electrical noise

Each piece of circuitry along the way adds a little more noise to the signal due to the thermally induced, random movement of electrons, but a well-designed circuit need add only a small amount of noise. While real life sound signals are always changing in level, the level of noise is essentially constant, so it's evident that if you feed a very low level audio signal into a circuit, the ratio of the noise to the wanted signal is going to be worse than if you feed in a strong signal.

The obvious way to minimise the percentage of noise added to a signal is to make sure the signal is at as high a level as possible, but there is also a limit to how high a signal level can be before it overloads the circuit its passing through. Overload causes the circuitry to clip the extremes of the incoming waveform and the result is audible distortion. Figure 2.4 shows a signal being clipped.

To avoid the twin evils of noise and clipping distortion, it is important to use the highest signal level possible while still leaving a little safety margin so that any unexpected peaks can pass through without being distorted. If you look at the VU meters on an analogue tape recorder, you'll see that the optimum operating level is the 0VU mark and the safety headroom is how far you can push the level beyond this point before you hear distortion. Figure 2.5 shows a realistic signal level with enough safety margin to accommodate unexpected signal peaks.

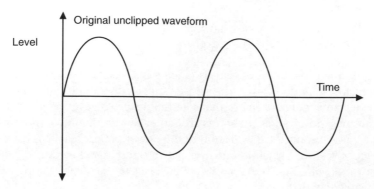

Original unclipped waveform

Level

Time

Figure 2.4: Effect of signal clipping

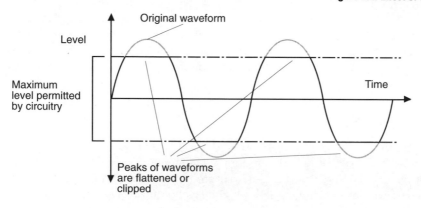

Original waveform

Level

Maximum
level permitted
by circuitry

Time

Peaks of waveforms
are flattened or
clipped

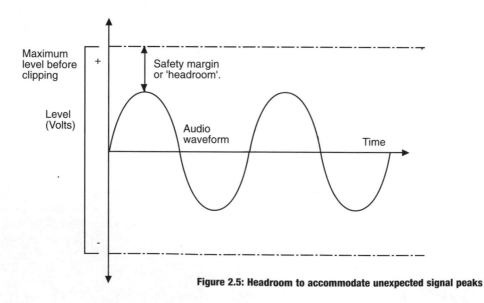

Maximum
level before
clipping

+

Safety margin
or 'headroom'.

Level
(Volts)

Audio
waveform

Time

-

Figure 2.5: Headroom to accommodate unexpected signal peaks

analogue and digital distortion

Most analogue circuits (and analogue tape for that matter) don't suddenly clip when the level gets too high but, instead, the amount of distortion increases progressively until all the headroom is used up, then clipping occurs. That's why the record level meters on an analogue tape recorder can occasionally be driven past the 0VU mark, up into the red. Distortion increases progressively as the signal level exceeds 0VU, but it's normally possible to go several dBs 'into the red' before the distortion is severe enough to become audible.

Digital circuits (and digital tape), on the other hand, have no safety margin or area of progressive distortion beyond 0VU, only clipping. For this reason, the nominal safe operating level for digital equipment is usually chosen around 12dB or so below the 0VU clipping point. Figure 2.6 shows how both analogue tape and digital systems respond to overload.

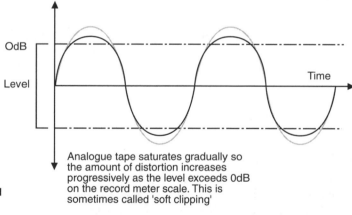

Analogue tape saturates gradually so the amount of distortion increases progressively as the level exceeds 0dB on the record meter scale. This is sometimes called 'soft clipping'

Figure 2.6: How analogue tape and digital systems overload

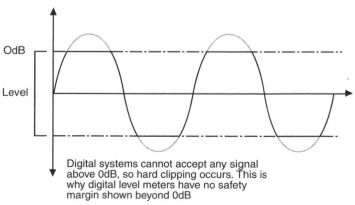

Digital systems cannot accept any signal above 0dB, so hard clipping occurs. This is why digital level meters have no safety margin shown beyond 0dB

If too small a signal is fed into a digital system, it is represented by fewer 'bits' which again results in noise, so just because something is digital doesn't mean the old analogue problems are left behind. With both analogue and digital recording, it is vital to set the right recording level in order to get the best possible sound with the least background noise. The basics of digital recording will be covered later in this book.

setting gain structure

Put simply, setting up your Gain Structure is ensuring that every piece of circuitry in your studio is running at its optimum signal level – not high enough to cause distortion, but not low enough to allow excessive noise to intrude. This means not only ensuring that your recording levels are optimised, but also the levels of any signals fed into your mixer, any signal processing equipment plugged into mixer, and any tape machines fed from your mixer. This may sound complicated, but it isn't really. You just have to be methodical and pay attention to setting up your system properly before you start recording.

Good gain structure starts right back at the microphone preamplifier of your mixer, tape deck or cassette multitracker, so if you have a mixer or multitrack workstation equipped with PFL (Pre Fade Listen), buttons, use these to monitor the individual inputs. By adjusting the input gain trim controls, you can get each signal reading an optimum level on the meters. This takes a few minutes but it's absolutely vital to a good recording. If you're not already familiar with these terms, see the chapter on mixers.

impedance

Electrical resistance is a familiar concept – the higher the resistance, the more voltage you need to force a given current through it. Resistance is measured in Ohms and most people will be familiar with Ohms' law. Ohms' law states that $R = V/I$ where V is the voltage across the circuit and I is the current (in Amps) flowing through it.

Impedance is essentially a circuit's resistance to an alternating current such as an audio signal. In a purely resistive circuit, resistance and impedance are the same thing, but in a reactive circuit containing capacitors or inductors, the impedance will vary depending on the frequency of the signal passing through it. Most audio equipment is designed so as to keep the impedance reasonably constant over the entire audio range but this isn't always possible in components such as loudspeakers.

Input impedance is, in effect, the load that a circuit presents to the device trying to feed a signal into it, but how is output impedance defined? Input impedance is related to how much electrical current is absorbed by a circuit whereas output impedance is related to how much current an output can supply. In order to get one piece of equipment to feed another without problems, we have to pay attention to impedance matching.

matching

In electrical terms, a matched connection is where a circuit with a given output impedance is feeding an input which has the same value input impedance. A 600 Ohm output feeding a 600 Ohm input would be a perfect match. This is an important concept in any system concerned with transferring the maximum amount of power from one circuit to another, the obvious example being an amplifier driving a loudspeaker. In mechanical terms, impedance matching can be thought of as the electrical equivalent of gear ratios in a car gear box.

With low level audio signals, we're no longer concerned about optimum power transfer – we simply want to get a signal from one place to another without doing it any damage. To achieve this, it's usual for the source impedance (the output impedance of the equipment providing the signal) to be made between five and ten times lower than the load impedance (the device accepting the signal). Not only does this prevent the signal from being unduly loaded, it also enables one source to drive two or three loads simultaneously.

To see how this works in practice, a mixing console has an input impedance of around 1 kOhm while a low-impedance dynamic microphone might have an impedance of 200 Ohms or so. This satisfies the criteria for a good match as the ratio is 5:1. Line inputs have a typical impedance of 50 kohms while most equipment designed to drive such a load will usually have an output impedance measured in hundreds of Ohms.

If the load impedance is considerably higher than the source impedance driving it, it should be possible to split the source signal to drive two or more loads. You can't, however, work the other way round by joining two outputs together to mix them. The two output stages will try to dominate each other and the signal may be seriously distorted. In some cases, equipment damage may result.

If this seems a bit academic, don't worry, because modern day recording equipment is invariably designed to interconnect without matching problems. If you have a cassette multitracker, you should read the handbook to find out if you need to work with high or low impedance microphones, but other than that, everything should work together quite comfortably. The basic rules on impedance matching are:

★ When transferring a signal from one device to another, the output impedance of the source device should be at least five times lower than the input impedance of the receiving device.

★ A signal output may be split to feed two inputs, but you should never use a Y lead to try to feed two outputs into one input. Two or more signals should only be mixed together using a mixer.

★ When connecting loudspeakers to amplifiers, the loudspeaker impedance should be as near as possible to the output impedance quoted for the amplifier.

There are two 'standard' operating levels in common usage, the -10dBV standard for semi-pro and domestic recording equipment, and the +4dBu standard for pro studio gear. These are close enough that as long as you set your gain controls correctly, they will usually still work together, though the meter readings between the two types of equipment will not agree. In theory, mixing pro and semi-pro equipment will compromise your gain structure slightly, but in practice, the deterioration in signal-to-noise ratio is insignificant.

decibels

Equipment specs quote them, meters read them and operating levels conform to them, but what is the decibel (dB) and where did it originate? Even though our VU meters are calibrated in decibels, even the most experienced engineer can start to fumble when asked to explain exactly what they are, and how they are related to terms like dBu, dBm, dBv and dBV. It's all a throwback to the pioneering days of telephones, but at least it's a standard – of sorts.

The term decibel means a tenth of a bel, the bel part being named after Alexander Graham Bell, hence the capital B in dB. dB doesn't necessarily relate to any fixed level of signal; it is most often used as a convenient way of expressing the ratio between two signal levels. The decibel scale is logarithmic, just like the human ear, so decibels on a VU meter correspond pretty closely to our subjective impression of loudness.

The method of calculating dBs for both voltage and power ratios is shown at the end of this chapter, and you might like to know that you can pick any power or voltage to be your 0dB reference level and then express all other values relative to that. For example, the record level meter on a tape machine is always set so that the optimum recording level is shown as 0dB, regardless of what that means in terms of magnetic flux at the record head. If a signal is lower than optimum, it is read as minus so many dBs, whereas if the signal is too high, it is shown as plus so many dBs.

Because dBs are logarithmic, most calculations involve addition or subtraction rather than multiplication or division. For example, a doubling of voltage corresponds to a 6dB increase, so making the voltage four times as big would equate to a 12dB increase. Another example? A voltage amplifier having a gain of 60dB amplifies the input signal 1000 times. The same is true of specifications such as dynamic range: 100dB dynamic range means that the largest signal a circuit can handle is 100,000 times bigger than the smallest signal it can handle.

dBm

While dBs express only ratios, the dBm is a fixed value where 0dBm equates to 1 milliwatt of power dissipated into a 600 Ohm load. This is of little direct relevance in the world of modern audio, but was vitally important in the pioneering days of telephone when small amounts of electrical power needed to be transmitted over long distances. 0dBm then, refers to a signal of 0.775 Volts applied to a load of 600 Ohms, which dissipates a power of 1 mW.

Today, the term dBm is often abused to signify a signal level of 0.775 Volts, but unless the load impedance is exactly 600 Ohms, this is technically incorrect. Because exact load impedances are less of an issue in modern audio systems, the new term dBu (u meaning unloaded) was introduced to signify a voltage level of 0.775 Volts, regardless of the load impedance. In other words, while the dBm is a measure of power, the dBu is a measure only of voltage. The term dBv (lower case v) also means the same thing as dBu, though the term dBu is more commonly used.

A standard reference voltage level of 0.775 Volts is pretty clumsy when 1 Volt would be easier to manage. That's where the recently introduced dBV (note the upper case V) comes in; it signifies a signal level of 1V without regard to the load impedance.

standard levels

You may have heard it said that some recording equipment works at 'Plus 4' or 'Minus 10', but what does that mean in practice? 'Plus 4' actually means +4dBu, an operating level adopted in pro audio due to historic rather than purely logical reasons, and corresponding to an RMS signal level of 1.23 Volts. This is a fairly convenient figure for use with modern op-amp circuitry as it leaves a sensible amount of headroom before the circuitry runs into clipping.

The so-called 'Minus 10' level was introduced along with semi-pro recording gear and is largely a Japanese concept. Correctly stated, this is -10dBV which corresponds to 0.316 Volts, or just under a third of a volt. Again this is reasonable for use with op-amp circuitry, but many purists feel the +4dBu system provides a better balance between noise and headroom.

Some musical instruments, such as electronic keyboards, have an even lower, -20dBV output level allowing them to be used with domestic hi-fi equipment. Because of this, some effects units also have matching -20dBV low level inputs corresponding to a signal level of only 0.1 Volt RMS. Such equipment can cause problems because a lot of mixer gain is required to bring the signal up to a manageable level, the unwanted side-effect being noise. For this reason, it may be wise to use purpose-built keyboard preamps or DI boxes rather than relying purely on the mixer line input to provide all the gain.

calculating dbs

When comparing two power levels, the number of dBs difference may be calculated by the equation:

Number of dBs = 10 log (P1/P2) where P1 and P2 are the two powers being compared and where the log is to the base 10.

If you don't understand how logs work, don't worry because few engineers actually get out their calculators when dealing with dBs. Instead, there are some useful figures that you should remember, the most common being that 3dB represents a doubling in power. It follows then that a 10 Watt amplifier can produce 3dB more power than a 5 Watt amplifier. Similarly, a 20 Watt amplifier can produce 3dB more power than a 10 Watt amplifier. So, how much more powerful is a 20 Watt amplifier than a 5 Watt amplifier? Simple, just add two lots of 3dB, which gives you 6dB.

Because of the mathematical relationship between power and voltage, the calculations are slightly different when it comes to working out voltage ratios in dBs. Here the equation is:

Number of dBs = 20 log (P1/P2) where P1 and P2 are the two powers being compared and where the log is to the base 10.

Note that we now have a 20 in the equation instead of a 10 which means the answer is twice what it would be for a ratio of powers. In other words, double the voltage and the level goes up by 6dB; halve the voltage and the level goes down by 6dB.

chapter 3

about mixers

Whether you use an all-in-one cassette multitracker or a separate multitrack recorder and mixer, the mixer is the hub of your studio – not only does it allow you to change the level and EQ of signals, it also provides a means of routing signals to and from tape, or to external effects and processors. In principle, a mixing console is pretty straightforward, though I'd agree that large studio consoles can be intimidating at first sight. Even so, the principles are the same, and the concepts embodied in a cassette multitracker's mixing section also apply to studio consoles.

Mixers comprise several identical 'building blocks' known as channels, and the purpose of a channel is to change the level of the signal fed into it, to enable the signal to be EQ'd, and to provide routing. Routing includes the ability to send the signal to what is known as a mix buss – an electrical circuit that allows the outputs from two or more channels to be added together to form a single, composite signal. To illustrate these concepts, I'll describe a simple, 4-channel mixer designed to mix four signals into one. Because the mixer has only one output, the output signal, in this case, will be mono. For stereo, we'd need two signal paths, one to carry the left speaker signal and one to carry the right speaker signal.

mic and line levels

Earlier, I emphasised that all electronic circuitry has an optimum operating range, and I introduced the idea of gain structure. Internally, mixers are designed to work within a particular range of signal levels, usually up to 10 or so Volts. Some signals, known as line level signals fall within this range, such as the outputs from effects units, tape machines and many electronic instruments, but the signal produced by a microphone is at a far lower level than this. To bring the mic level up to the internal line level used by the mixer, there's a low-noise microphone amplifier, right at the input of the channel, and this may also be fitted with phantom power circuitry enabling it to be used with capacitor microphones.

Capacitor microphones require power to operate, and phantom power is simply a standard method of sending 48 Volts along the mic cable from the mixing console. Phantom powering can only be used with balanced microphones. As a rule, if the mic body is fitted with a three-pin XLR socket, it is balanced, but always check the data sheet that came with the mic to be sure. Use of unbalanced cables might cause damage to dynamic mics, as could plugging or unplugging them with the phantom power turned on. You can find out more about microphones in the chapter Microphone Types.

channel gain

Because not all microphones produce the same level of output, and because the output level depends on how close and how loud the sound being recorded is, the microphone amplifier is invariably equipped with a gain control which determines the amount of amplification applied to the signal. In other words, the setting of the gain control relates to how much bigger the signal will be made. Line level signals don't need to pass through the microphone amplifier, so mixer channels also have a line input. Normally only the line or mic input may be used, not both at once.

The line input on a typical mixer will also be fitted with a gain control, and on most professional mixers, the mic and line inputs will have separate gain controls, but on most home recording mixers and multitrackers, a common control is used for both mic and line gain adjustment.

mixer channels

Figure 3.1 shows a simplified schematic of a 4-channel, mono mixer with simple bass and treble equalisation. Separate mic and line gain controls have been shown to aid clarity, but in practice, a single, shared control is more likely on a mixer of this type. There are separate input sockets for both the microphone and line input signals though on budget equipment, it is possible that a single socket will be used for both. A switch is sometimes used to select between the microphone input and the line input, but not always.

After the input gain stage comes the equalisation section which can be as simple as the bass/treble (also known as Hi\Lo) arrangement shown here, or can be a complex, multi-band affair, as is more common in serious semi-pro and professional mixers. For more about EQ see the chapter Equalisation. More sophisticated mixers have an additional switch allowing the equalisation section to be bypassed when not in use.

Finally the signal level is controlled by a knob or fader before it passes to the mix buss, sometimes via an On or Mute switch. Note that all four input

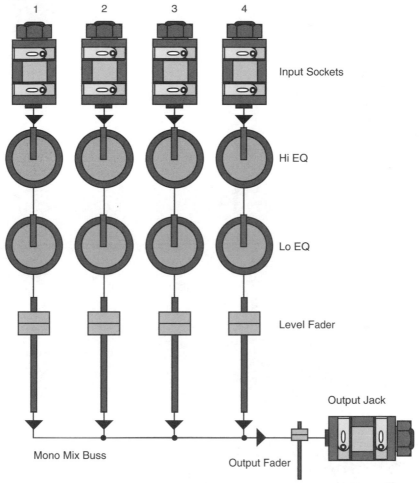

Figure 3.1: Simplified 4-channel, mono mixer

channels are identical, and a larger mixer would have more input channels.

The combined signal on the mix buss passes through further amplification stages (known as the mix amplifier) controlled by the a master level fader or knob. This controls the output level of the mixer, allowing it to present the correct signal level to the amplifier or tape recorder connected to the mixer. The master fader may also be used to make controlled fades at the end of songs.

stereo mixers

A stereo mixer is only slightly more complicated than a mono mixer as can be seen from Figure 3.2. This is very similar to the mixer shown in Figure 3.1,

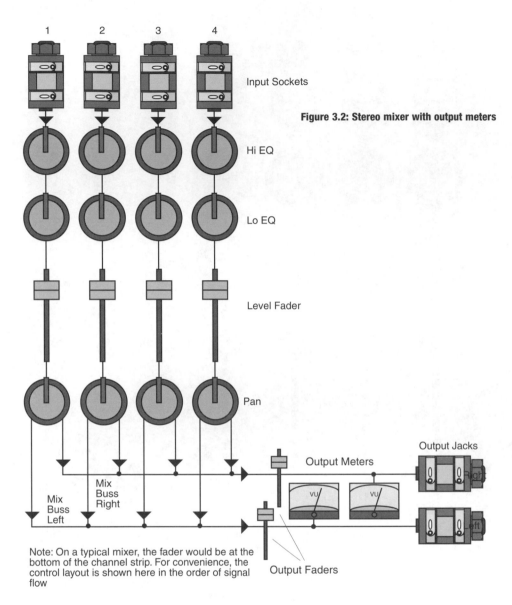

Figure 3.2: Stereo mixer with output meters

1 2 3 4

Input Sockets

Hi EQ

Lo EQ

Level Fader

Pan

Mix Buss Left

Mix Buss Right

Output Meters

Output Jacks

Output Faders

Note: On a typical mixer, the fader would be at the bottom of the channel strip. For convenience, the control layout is shown here in the order of signal flow

except that the input channels have an extra control for panning the signal between the mixer's left and right outputs. When the pan control is turned completely anti-clockwise, the channel signal is routed exclusively to the left mix buss; turning it clockwise routes the signal to the right buss. Leaving the pan control in the centre routes equal amounts of signal to the left and right busses, making the resulting sound (when reproduced over a stereo speaker system) appear to originate from midway between the speakers. These two busses are often referred to in the singular as a stereo mix buss, though in reality, the busses are physically separate.

In a stereo mixer, there are two master faders, one for the left output and one for the right, though some mixers use a single stereo control to save on cost and space. Figure 3.2 also shows a stereo level meter, which allows the user to monitor the output level of the mixer. This will be familiar to anyone who has used a stereo cassette recorder, though the mechanism could take the form of a moving-coil meter with a physical pointer or it could be a row of LEDs (Light Emitting Diodes) arranged in the form of a ladder.

This type of simple mixer so far described is much like those used in small PA applications, though the mixer section of a cassette multitracker isn't very different. A stereo mixer of this type is usually described in the form 'something' into two; for example, a twelve into two (12:2) mixer has twelve input channels and two (left and right) outputs.

auxiliaries

In the studio, we don't just want to mix and EQ signals, we also want to do things like add effects or send a mix to the performer's headphones. In a live situation, a cue mix is required to feed to the stage monitors, and there has to be some way of providing a different balance on the cue output than on the main stereo mix outputs. For example, singers usually need to hear more of the vocals than of the instrumental backing.

pre-fade send

Both effects and cue (sometimes called foldback) monitoring can be handled using the auxiliary controls on a mixer, and Figure 3.3 shows how these fit into the picture. Here you can see two new controls: Aux 1 and Aux 2, where aux is short for auxiliary. Aux 1 is simply another level control feeding a mono mix buss which runs across the mixer to the Aux 1 Master level control and then to the Aux 1 output socket, but the signal feeding the Aux 1 control is taken before the channel fader and so is known as a pre-fade send. The implication of this is that the Aux 1 signal level doesn't change if the channel fader is adjusted. In other words, any mix set up using the pre-fade aux send will be completely independent of the channel faders. This is just what we want for setting up a cue mix for the musician or singer doing an overdub. The overall Aux 1 mix is controlled by the Aux 1 Master level control, and the Aux 1 output would normally feed a headphone amplifier. Using a pre-fade send, the engineer can provide the musician with a monitor mix that is exactly to his or her liking.

post-fade send

The second aux control, Aux 2, takes its feed from after the channel fader

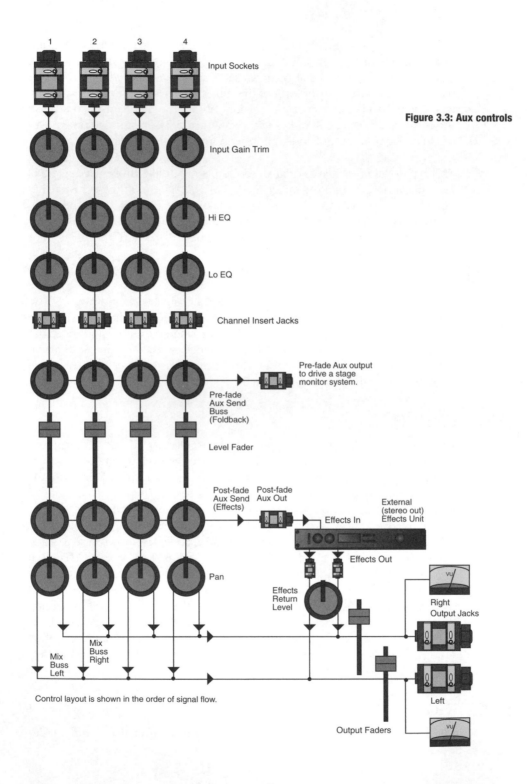

Figure 3.3: Aux controls

Input Sockets

Input Gain Trim

Hi EQ

Lo EQ

Channel Insert Jacks

Pre-fade Aux output to drive a stage monitor system.

Pre-fade Aux Send Buss (Foldback)

Level Fader

Post-fade Aux Send (Effects)

Post-fade Aux Out

External (stereo out) Effects Unit

Effects In

Effects Out

Pan

Effects Return Level

VU

Right Output Jacks

Mix Buss Right

Mix Buss Left

Left

VU

Control layout is shown in the order of signal flow.

Output Faders

40

(post-fader), so its level is affected by any changes in the channel fader setting. This is exactly what we need if Aux 2 is being used to feed an external effect, such as reverb, because when the channel signal level is turned up or down, we want the amount of effect to change by a corresponding amount.

By using different settings of the Aux 2 control on each channel, it is possible to send different amounts of each channel's signal to the same effects unit. When the output from this effects unit is added to the main stereo mix, this has the advantage that different amounts of the same effect can be added to different sounds in a mix. A typical example might be where one reverberation unit is used to provide a rich reverb for the vocals, less reverb for the drums and little or none for the guitars and bass.

It is important to note that an effects unit used in conjunction with a channel aux send should be set up so that it produces only the effected sound and none of the original. This is usually accomplished by means of a mix control, which is either in the form of a knob or accessed via the effects unit's editing software. In either case, the mix should be set to 100% effect, 0% dry.

effects returns

The output of the effect unit may be fed back into the mixer via spare input channels or via dedicated effects return inputs, also known as aux returns. Aux returns are electrically similar to input channels but usually sport fewer facilities. They will have no mic inputs, and on a simple mixer, they may have no EQ and no aux sends of their own. Normally they feed straight into the main stereo mix.

A spare input channel (or pair panned hard left and right for stereo) may be used as an effect return, and here you gain the benefit of EQ and access to the aux send busses (for example, you may want to add reverb to the cue mix), but you must ensure that the corresponding aux send (in this case Aux 2) is turned down on the return channel, otherwise the effect signal will be fed back on itself, resulting in an unpleasant howl or scream. The diagram in Figure 3.3 also shows how an external effects unit is connected. All the controls shown in the figures are arranged in a logical order to illustrate the signal flow through the channel, though commercial mixers tend to have the pan and aux controls located above the channel fader for convenience.

insert points

Another way to connect an effects unit or signal processor to a mixer is via an Insert Point. All serious stand-alone mixers have insert points on the

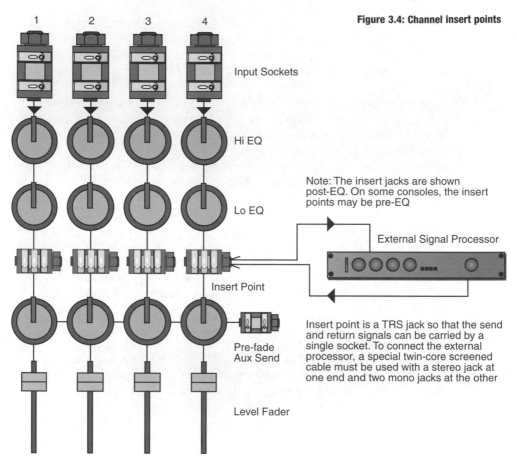

Figure 3.4: Channel insert points

1   2   3   4

Input Sockets

Hi EQ

Lo EQ

Note: The insert jacks are shown post-EQ. On some consoles, the insert points may be pre-EQ

External Signal Processor

Insert Point

Pre-fade Aux Send

Insert point is a TRS jack so that the send and return signals can be carried by a single socket. To connect the external processor, a special twin-core screened cable must be used with a stereo jack at one end and two mono jacks at the other

Level Fader

Pan control and busses omitted for clarity

input channels and also on the master stereo outputs, though self-contained multitrackers don't always have them. An insert point is just a socket that allows the normal channel or stereo master signal path to be interrupted and re-routed through an external device. When no plug is inserted, spring contacts inside the socket complete the connection so that the signal flow is not broken.

On most home recording mixers, the insert points are on stereo jack sockets, which means you need a specially wired Y lead or adaptor to be able to use them. The stereo socket is conventionally wired 'Tip Send/Ring Return', with the cable screen being common to both send and return. Figure 3.4 shows the channel insert points in a typical mixer. Physically, they appear as stereo jacks and are usually found near to the mic and line input sockets.

effects and processors

This next paragraph is very important, and understanding its implications will save you a lot of trouble and frustration later on. While it is permissible to connect any type of effect or signal processor via an insert point, there are restrictions on what can be used via the aux send/return system. As a rule of thumb, only delay-based effects such as reverb, echo, chorus, phasing, flanging and pitch shifting should be connected via the aux system, and these are generally called effects. If the box uses delay to do its work, it's an effect, and if there's a dry/effect mix knob or parameter, the box is almost certain to be an effect. The unique thing about an effect is that it is added to the original signal. A process, such as EQ, doesn't add to the original signal, but rather changes the original signal. Processors such as compressors, gates and EQ may only be connected via insert points, and under normal circumstances, never via the aux sends and returns.

multitrack mixers

Cassette multitrackers have relatively simple mixer sections, and because everything is in one box, you don't have any wiring to worry about other than plugging in the mics. Things get slightly more complicated when you move up to a separate mixer and multitrack recorder, but most of what you've learned already still applies.

As touched upon earlier, a studio console doesn't just mix signals, it also acts as a central routing system, sending signals to the different tape machine tracks, adding effects from external processors, and mixing the outputs from the tape machine to produce a final, stereo mix. At the same time, it has to function as a 'mixer within a mixer' so that a separate control room monitor mix can be set up while the performers are recording or overdubbing.

tracks or channels?

The terminology associated with mixers can be a little confusing, and a common mistake that even experienced users make is to refer to a mixer as having so many 'tracks'. In fact mixers don't have tracks, they have channels (inputs), and Groups (outputs). Tape recorders have tracks!

So far we've described a simple input channel with input gain, EQ, aux sends, pan control and a fader, but on a multitrack mixer there are two different kinds of channel. The main Input channel generally has the most comprehensive facilities and is used to feed microphones and line level sources such as keyboards and samplers into the mixer while recording.

When you're mixing your tape tracks, the input channels handle the output from the multitrack tape machine.

The other type of channel is the Monitor channel, so-called because it is used to set up a guide monitor mix based on the multitrack outputs while the performers are overdubbing new parts. Without some way of hearing a mix of the tracks that have already be recorded, there would be no way for the musician to keep time, or stay in tune with the music already recorded.

monitor channels

Monitor channels tend to have fewer facilities than the main Input channels, because their main job is to provide a rough mix during the session. They may have little or no EQ and fewer aux sends than the main channel, though on an in-line mixer (so-called because the main Input and Monitor controls are located in the same channel strip as the input channel controls), there's often provision to switch all or part of the EQ between the main and Monitor signal paths, and the same is often true of the aux sends. To make visualisation easier, I like to think of the monitor section as being like a separate mixer connected to the tape machine outputs. The fact that this shares the same box as the main mixer (used for feeding stuff onto tape), is purely for convenience.

Because there is no need for a monitor mix when the recording is complete, most mixers allow the Monitor channels to be used as extra line inputs at the mixing stage. These may be used as additional effects returns or to add sequenced MIDI instruments, and they generally feed directly into the stereo mix.

groups

Up until now, we've talked about mixers with simple stereo outputs, but for multitrack work, we need some way to route different signals to different multitrack inputs at the same time. That's where the mixer Group comes in. Whereas a stereo mixer just has a left and a right output, a multitrack mixer has several additional outputs, each with its own fader. These separate outputs are known as Groups, and for use with an 8-track tape recorder, an 8-Group mixer is ideal. The term 8-Group simply means that the mixer has eight mix outputs in addition to the main stereo output. You may also see such a mixer described as an 8-buss console because the eight Groups are fed from eight mix busses.

Any of the Input channels may be routed to any of the eight Group outputs via routing switches linked to the eight Group busses (as well as to the stereo output), and if two or more channels are routed to the same output, they are automatically mixed together. As before, the channel faders set the relative levels of the various elements in the mix, but now the Group fader controls the overall level feeding the tape machine or other multitrack device. During recording, the Group outputs feed directly into the correspondingly numbered inputs of the multitrack tape machine, enabling any mixer input to be routed to any tape track without the need to re-plug any cables.

routing

On a cassette multitracker, routing the desired input signals to tape is relatively straightforward as you usually have only four tracks to play with. On a multitrack mixing console however, you'll find a set of routing buttons next to the channel faders, which are used to send the channel signals either to the various Group outputs (which are connected to the multitrack inputs) or to the stereo mix. At mixdown, the stereo mix is used to feed the stereo mastering recorder, but the stereo output also feeds the control monitor during recording, overdubbing and mixing so you can hear what you're working on.

pan and routing

Within each input channel, a single routing button handles the routing for a pair of Groups, with the Pan control being used to change the balance of what is sent to the odd and even numbered Groups. If you want to route a channel only to output Group 2, for example, you'd press the routing button marked 1,2 and turn the Pan control fully clockwise so that all the signal went to Group 2 and none to Group 1. Leaving the Pan in its centre position would send equal amounts of signal to Groups 1 and 2. To record something in stereo (for example, the different drum mics over a drum kit), the relevant channels would be routed to a pair of Groups and the Pan control used to position the various sounds between them. The outputs from these two Groups would then be recorded to two tracks of tape. When mixing, these two tape tracks would be panned hard left and right to maintain the stereo image you created while recording.

routing buttons

On an 8-Group mixer (the most popular format for project studio use) the routing buttons would be marked 1,2 3,4 5,6 7,8, with a further L,R button for routing the channel directly to the stereo mix. Figure 3.5 shows the signal flow through the routing buttons of a typical console including the signal path to the Group fader and Group output socket. Note that you don't have to use an 8-Group mixer to work with an 8-track tape machine, you could

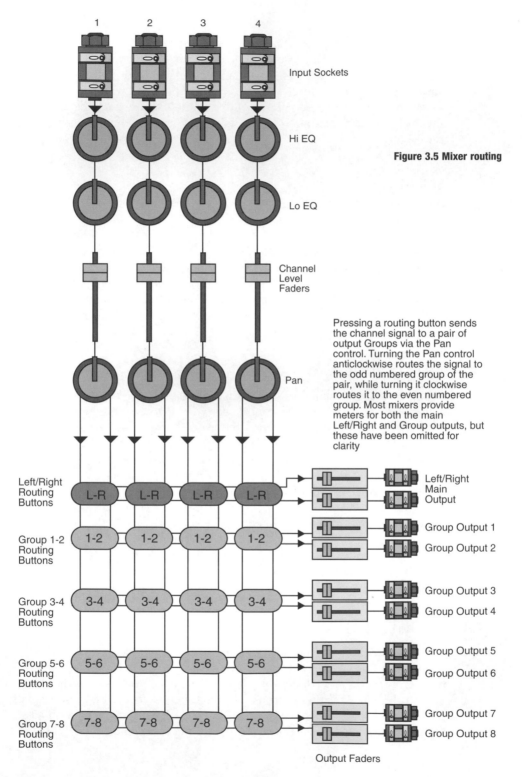

Figure 3.5 Mixer routing

Pressing a routing button sends the channel signal to a pair of output Groups via the Pan control. Turning the Pan control anticlockwise routes the signal to the odd numbered group of the pair, while turning it clockwise routes it to the even numbered group. Most mixers provide meters for both the main Left/Right and Group outputs, but these have been omitted for clarity

Input Channels   L-R Meters   Group Output Meters

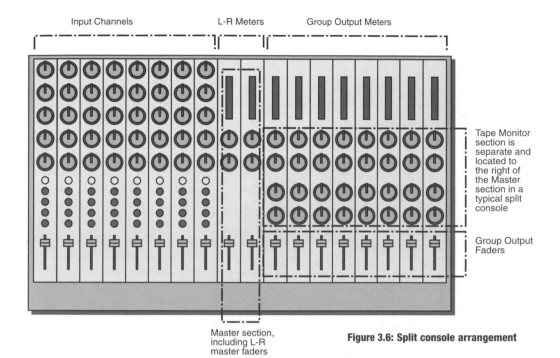

Tape Monitor
section is
separate and
located to
the right of
the Master
section in a
typical split
console

Group Output
Faders

Master section,
including L-R
master faders

Figure 3.6: Split console arrangement

use a 4-Group mixer so long as you don't need to record more than four Groups at a time. You can still record more than four tape tracks at a time by using channel direct outputs, insert sends or even spare aux sends to feed additional tape tracks.

By connecting Group output 1 to tape inputs 1 and 5, Group output 2 to tape inputs 2 and 6 and so on, you can still record on all eight tracks without having to replug any cables. The tape machine record status buttons determine which of the two possible tracks each Group will record onto.

split and in-line monitoring

On a conventional 'split' mixing console, the Group faders and the monitor channel controls are situated on the right hand side of the mixer. Between the main Input channels and the Monitor section is the Master section, which includes functions such as the master stereo faders, the aux send and aux return master controls. On a more advanced mixer, you'll also find things like the test oscillator, the talkback mic, Mix/2-Track monitoring, headphone level control and so on. An 8-Group console needs a minimum of eight monitor channels to provide an off-tape monitor mix, but many models have 16, allowing the mixer to be used with a 16-track recorder using the split wiring arrangement described in Figure 3.6. The basic requirements for a monitor channel are Level and Pan controls so that a stereo cue mix can

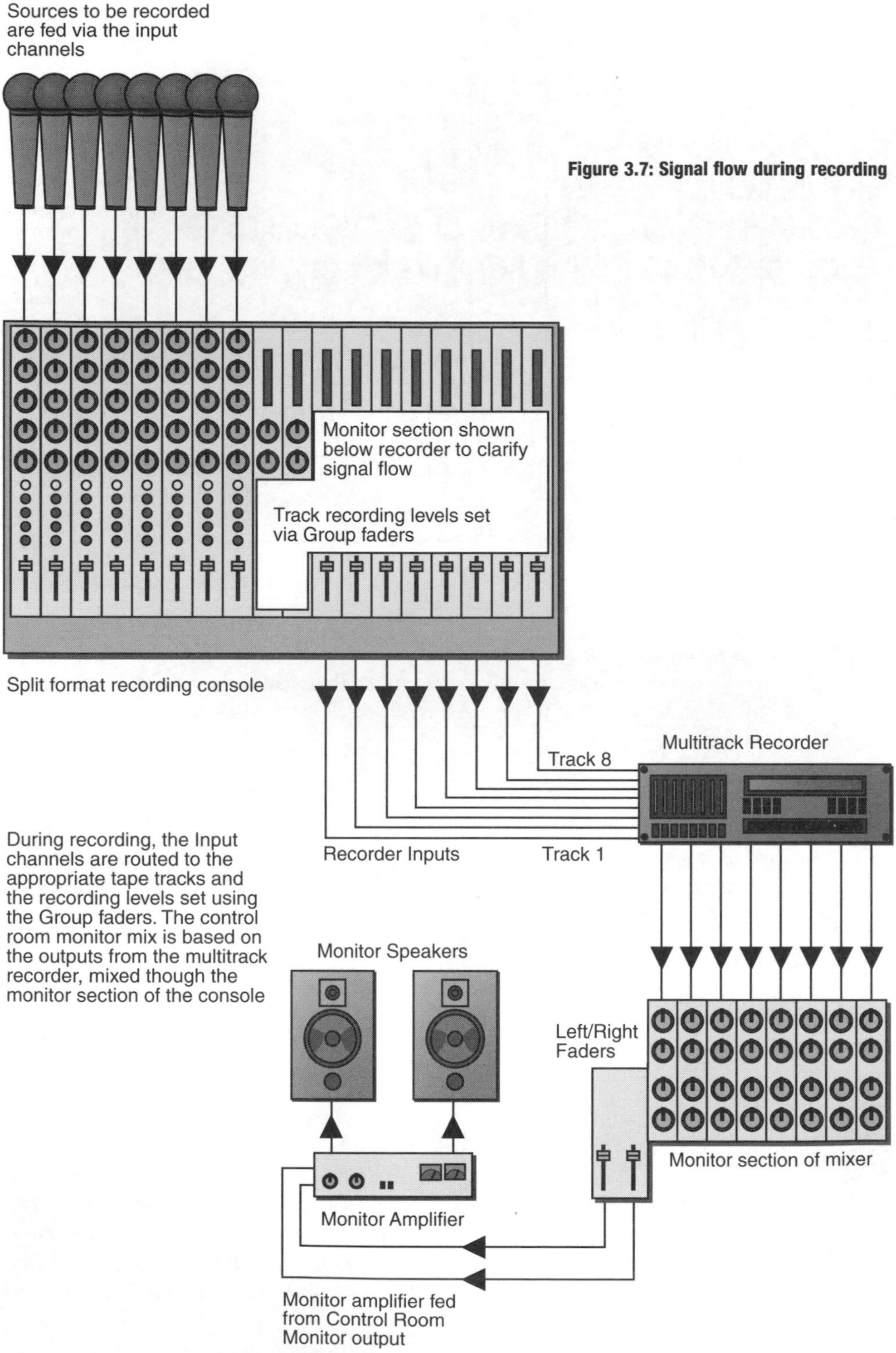

Sources to be recorded
are fed via the input
channels

Figure 3.7: Signal flow during recording

Monitor section shown
below recorder to clarify
signal flow

Track recording levels set
via Group faders

Split format recording console

Multitrack Recorder

Track 8

During recording, the Input
channels are routed to the
appropriate tape tracks and
the recording levels set using
the Group faders. The control
room monitor mix is based on
the outputs from the multitrack
recorder, mixed though the
monitor section of the console

Recorder Inputs

Track 1

Monitor Speakers

Left/Right
Faders

Monitor section of mixer

Monitor Amplifier

Monitor amplifier fed
from Control Room
Monitor output

48

be provided from the outputs of the multitrack recorder. In practice though, most monitor channels have some form of basic EQ and also have aux controls that feed the same aux busses as the main mixer Input channels. Figure 3.7 shows a multitrack mixer with the monitor section shown separately. In reality, the monitor section is housed in the same box as the rest of the mixer, but it can help to visualise it as a separate mixer within a mixer. The diagram shows the signal flow during recording.

tape monitoring

Why is it that the monitor section always monitors the tape machine outputs? What happens if you want to hear what you're playing at the same time as you're recording? Fortunately, modern multitrack tape machines are far simpler than they used to be when there was a time delay between the record and playback head and when there were separate switches on the tape machine to switch each tape track between input, sync and playback monitor mode.

Modern tape machines take care of monitor switching without you even having to think about it, and the relevant signal is always present at the tape output socket. If a track is being recorded, you hear the tape input, but if the track is in playback mode, you hear what's on tape. However, older tape machines usually have a switch which allows each monitor channel to be fed from either the multitrack output or the Group output (which is the same thing as the multitrack input).

console formats

Currently, virtually all budget recording consoles adopt the in-line format, which differs from the split concept in that the Monitor controls reside in the same channel strip as the main Input channel controls. In a split console, the monitor section is usually in the master section or to the right of it, giving it more of a separate feel. In-line consoles may seem confusing at first, but the advantage is that instead of being limited to just eight or 16 Monitor channels, there's one Monitor channel for every Input channel. This layout usually results in a mixer that is deeper front to back than an equivalent split design, but it also means the mixer can be made less wide for the same number of channels – an important consideration in a studio where space is limited.

split eq and aux sends

Most Monitor channels have at least one aux send control so that effects may be added to the foldback or cue mix, but there may be little or no room for EQ controls. Depending on the model and make of in-line mixer, you may get just a simple bass and treble EQ or no EQ at all. To help compensate, there's often a switching arrangement that allows the Monitor channel to share part of the main Input channel's EQ. For example, if the main EQ is a 4-band affair with two sweep mids, the Monitor channel may be able to make use of the Hi and Lo EQ leaving the main Input channel with two sweeps. In such cases, the sweep range is usually wide enough to allow the two mids to cover the entire audio spectrum.

Another common arrangement is for a couple of the aux sends to be switchable between either the Input or Monitor channel.

mixing down

When mixing down with a split console, you have to route all the tape tracks to the main Input channels and then set up the mix from scratch. With an in-line console, however, as each tracks is recorded, you can operate a 'flip' switch in the channel strip, which routes the tape signal through the main Input channel path leaving the Monitor input free for later use. The benefit of working this way is that you can be working on your mix and fine tuning the balance and EQ as you go along. By the time you've finished recording, you should already have the basis of a good mix set up.

monitors as line-ins

Once the flip switch has been operated, the monitor channels are connected to the console line inputs allowing many line level sources to be fed into the mix. In these days of large MIDI systems, many of which are used synced to tape, these additional inputs are a necessity, not a luxury. Furthermore, these spare Monitor channels may be used to handle extra effects returns if you run out of conventional effects return inputs. It's worth reiterating at this point that an effects return is just another kind of Input channel.

'all input' mixing

Though both in-line and split consoles have separate Monitor channels to provide an off-tape control room mix while recording, it seems that a great many people don't use them for that purpose at all. Instead they operate their mixers in so called 'all-input' mode.

If you have an 8-track tape machine, and providing you have enough mixer

Input channels, you can leave the outputs of your tape machine permanently connected to the first eight channels of the mixer, routing these directly to the stereo L/R mix. The remaining channels may then be used to handle the signals being recorded. This does away with the need to switch the off-tape signals between the Monitor and Input channels and also means that you can build up your mix, complete with added effects, as you record. In effect, your control room mix also becomes your final mix.

The permanently redundant Monitor channels may be used as inputs for MIDI instruments being sequenced in sync with the multitrack recorder or as effects returns. The only limitation of working this way, other than having to ensure you have a mixer with enough Input channels, is that the Monitor channels can't be routed via the Groups to create Subgroups – they always feed directly into the stereo L/R mix. There's no right or wrong way to use your console – it's just a matter of finding a system that works for you.

subgrouping

Just as the monitor channels change roles when switching from recording to mixing, so does the Group routing system. During recording, the Groups are used to route signals to tape, but when you mix, they can be routed back into the stereo mix. As always, there's a very good reason.

Imagine you have backing vocals recorded over four or five tracks of your multitrack tape. To change the overall level of the backing vocals, you'd have to change the level by moving several faders at once, which is both cumbersome and inaccurate. A more effective approach is to create a 'Subgroup' of the backing vocals by routing the vocal channels to a pair of Groups rather than directly to the Left/Right mix. This way, the whole stereo backing vocal mix can be controlled by just two Group faders. Some consoles have the Groups permanently routed to the stereo mix while others provide 'Groups to Stereo' buttons for each Group fader, and these generally route all odd-numbered Group faders to the left and all even-numbered ones to the right.

A better system, which is usually missing from budget consoles for cost reasons, is to provide Group Pan controls. If you have Group pan controls, you can create mono Subgroups and still pan them anywhere in the stereo mix. If you don't have Group Pan controls, you always have to use up two Group faders for every Subgrouping operation apart from those where the end result will be panned either hard left or hard right.

In a typical mix, you might create Subgroups from things like drums, backing vocals and keyboards, which reduces the number of faders which need to be moved during the mix. Note that any effects that are to be added to these Subgroups using the aux sends should be returned to the same Subgroup (using the channel or effect return routing buttons), otherwise the effect level won't change when the Group fader is moved. Figure 3.8 shows the signal flow at mixdown. In this example, the Monitor channels are being used as extra line inputs and the signal flow shows how Subgroups actually work.

choosing a mixer

When choosing a mixer as part of your system, don't look at your system as it is now but as it might be in a year or two's time. If you don't, you're bound to run out of channels as your MIDI system expands or as you add more tape tracks. If you have a very large MIDI set-up, consider whether buying a separate rack submixer would make more sense than buying one big multitrack console, and ask whether expander modules are available for the mixers on your short list. If you've moved into digital multitrack you have the option of using multiple machines to provide more tracks, but will your choice of mixer allow for this? You may even be considering mix automation, in which case, is there a system that can be added to your mixer at a later date?

You can never predict every future requirement, and even if you could, you probably couldn't afford to buy a mixer that would cover every eventuality, but a little forethought will help you choose something that you aren't likely to have to sell at a loss in six months' time when you've outgrown it.

digital mixers

Digital mixers do essentially the same job as their analogue counterparts, the main practical difference being the user interface. There may also be a digital link between the mixer and compatible digital multitrack machines which preserves signal integrity and simplifies wiring.

Because digital mixers can incorporate more features than analogue consoles, it would be impractical to provide a physical control for each function. Instead, there tends to be a physical fader for each channel, often motorised in the case of an automated mixer, but only one set of EQ and aux send controls. A selector button by each fader allows the control section to become active for that particular channel, and a display screen usually provides further information as well as a physical representation of some of the virtual controls.

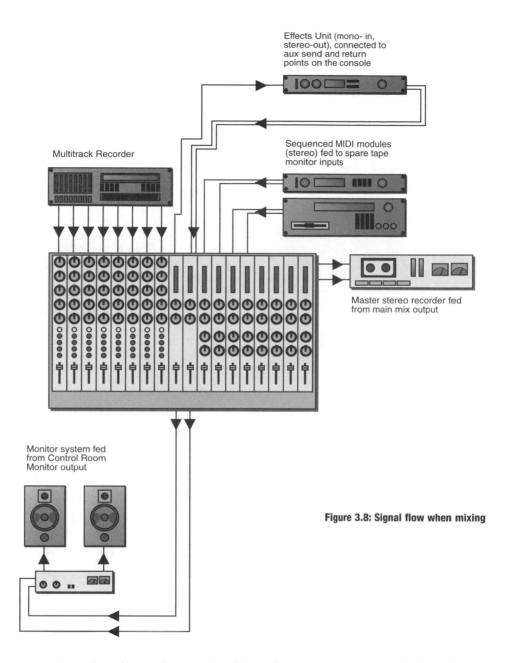

Effects Unit (mono- in, stereo-out), connected to aux send and return points on the console

Sequenced MIDI modules (stereo) fed to spare tape monitor inputs

Multitrack Recorder

Master stereo recorder fed from main mix output

Monitor system fed from Control Room Monitor output

Figure 3.8: Signal flow when mixing

Most digital consoles include effects, dynamic processing and the ability to automate complete mixes, right down to EQ and aux settings, making it possible to recall an old mix many months later and get it back exactly as it was. Only a couple of years ago, I would have thought digital mixers beyond the scope of this book, but now they're already starting to appear in digital multitracker type products.

digital advantages

It's arguable whether digital mixers have any sonic advantage over analogue consoles, and they're certainly less straightforward to use, but they do make it possible to access and automate a great number of functions at a relatively low cost and in a very compact form. Already we've almost reached the stage where it is cheaper for a manufacturer to build a completely automated digital mixer than an equivalent manually operated analogue mixer.

One very real advantage of using a digital mixer with a digital multitrack recorder is that the signal is kept in the digital domain for as long as possible. Indeed, using a digital master recorder (such as a DAT machine), once the mic signal has been recorded to digital, it need never leave the digital domain again until it reaches the end user's hi-fi system. As a rule, signal deterioration occurs whenever analogue signals are converted to digital signals or vice versa, so once a signal is in the digital domain, it makes sense to keep it there.

chapter 4

microphone types

Every microphone performs the same basic task of converting sound energy into electrical energy, but there are many different types of microphone and one of the recording engineer's many skills is knowing how to pick the best type for a particular job. If the right choice is to be made, it helps to have a basic knowledge of how microphones work and in what areas the various types differ.

In music recording, we encounter mainly dynamic or capacitor microphones, dynamic mics being the most common because of their suitability to stage work. In professional applications, you may also come across ribbon microphones, favoured for classical music applications, but ribbon mics are very rarely seen outside of professional studios or broadcast companies

One factor all microphones have in common is that the air vibrations that constitute sound are used to move a lightweight diaphragm, the movement of which is then used to generate an equivalent electrical signal. To put it more directly, the rapid positive and negative air pressure changes which we perceive as sound are converted by the microphone into analogous positive and negative fluctuations in electrical current.

dynamic mics

A dynamic mic comprises a lightweight, rigid diaphragm attached to a coil of wire suspended in a magnetic field created by a permanent magnet and an air gap. As the diaphragm moves in response to sound, so does the coil, and a tiny electrical current is generated in exactly the same way as spinning a dynamo produces electricity. Faraday's laws dictate that moving an electrical conductor in a magnetic field will cause an electrical current to flow in that conductor – which is exactly what happens when the diaphragm (and hence the coil) is set in motion by a sound. Dynamic mics are relatively inexpensive, mechanically robust, and require no electrical power to operate, which makes them attractive for many home recording applications.

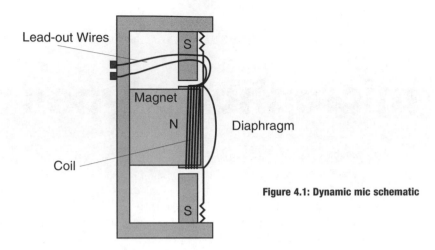

Lead-out Wires

Magnet

N

Diaphragm

Coil

Figure 4.1: Dynamic mic schematic

On the other hand, the sound energy has to move both the microphone's diaphragm and the coil attached to it, the outcome of which is that high frequency vibrations are opposed by the combined inertia of the coil and diaphragm. Inertia resists acceleration and a vibrating microphone diaphragm has to accelerate and decelerate many times each second as the diaphragm moves first one way and then the other. In practical terms, this means that dynamic models are struggling pretty hard by the time you get to the upper frequencies of the human hearing range and few models produce a meaningful output far beyond 16kHz. Figure 4.1 shows a typical dynamic mic schematic.

Another side-effect of the finite mass of the diaphragm/coil assembly is that the dynamic microphone is not particularly efficient – the signal needs to be amplified many times before it is large enough to be usable. Unfortunately, the more you have to amplify a signal, the more electrical background noise is added. With loud or nearby sounds, this presents no problem, but when working with quiet or distant sound sources, the dynamic microphone copes less well.

The ribbon mic is a form of dynamic microphone, except that the diaphragm and voice coil are replaced by a thin metal ribbon suspended in a magnetic field. In this type of microphone, the ribbon moves in response to sound energy and the resulting electrical signal is induced in the ribbon itself. The ribbon is lighter than the combined voice-coil and diaphragm assembly of a conventional dynamic microphone, which makes it slightly better able to cope with high frequencies, though the main advantage of ribbon microphones is their smooth, detailed sound.

capacitor mics

Capacitor microphones, sometimes also known as condenser mics, have been around for decades, but they still represent the state of the art in microphone technology. Capacitor mics don't need voice coils because they work on an entirely different principle. This means the diaphragm can be made much thinner and more flexible, and because of its lower inertia, the diaphragm is able to follow high frequencies with ease.

In practice, the diaphragm is just a few microns thick, and this is given a metal coating only a few atoms thick in order to make it electrically conductive. Holes are drilled in the fixed back-plate to prevent air being trapped between the plate – trapped air would tend to act as a cushion pushing against the moving diaphragm and adversely affecting the microphone's performance. The result is a very sensitive microphone capable of resolving high frequency detail right up to the limits of human hearing and beyond.

As the diaphragm vibrates, its distance from the stationary metal plate varies, and if a fixed electrical charge is applied between the diaphragm and the plate, a corresponding change in electrical voltage is produced. This voltage change is amplified by circuitry within the microphone, which is why capacitor microphones need electrical power to operate. Power is also needed to provide the electrical charge on the diaphragm. Figure 4.2 shows how a capacitor mic works.

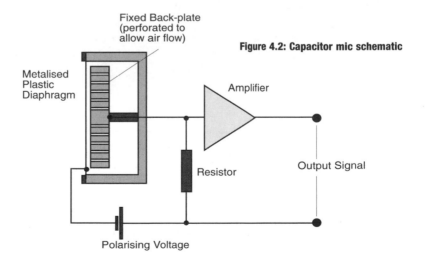

Fixed Back-plate (perforated to allow air flow)

Figure 4.2: Capacitor mic schematic

Metalised Plastic Diaphragm

Amplifier

Resistor

Output Signal

Polarising Voltage

While the principle of operation of all capacitor mics is the same, they can be built with different size diaphragms, different thickness diaphragms, and diaphragms made of different materials. Small-diaphragm models tend to sound extremely accurate while large-diaphragm models often have a warm, flattering sound making them popular for studio vocals.

capacitor pros and cons

Capacitor mics exhibit a significant increase in sensitivity compared with dynamic models making them more suitable for recording both quiet and distant sources. They can also resolve high frequency detail up to and beyond the limit of human hearing. If they're so good, why use anything else?

Capacitor microphones need an internal preamplifier in order to amplify the signal from the capsule, and to provide impedance matching. This adds to the manufacturing cost and a source of power is needed, not only to run the preamp, but also to provide the electrical charge on the diaphragm. The most common source of microphone power is the 48V phantom power source built into most mixing consoles, though tube-based capacitor mics tend to have their own dedicated power supplies.

Because of their complexity, good capacitor microphones are significantly more expensive than their dynamic counterparts and tend to be less robust. However, they are much more sensitive making them suitable for recording both quiet and distant sources and they can resolve high frequency detail much better than a dynamic microphone.

The broader market created by the project studio has meant that lower cost capacitor models are now available, some of which rival the professional models in terms of performance.

electret mics

A variation on the capacitor mic is the electret, where instead of the capsule being charged from an external voltage supply, the diaphragm contains a permanent electrical charge sealed in an insulating material. A preamplifier is still required to amplify the signal from the capsule, but this may be battery operated in some models.

The original electret mics performed quite poorly for the simple reason that building a diaphragm that could hold a magnetic charge meant making it thicker and heavier than that on a true capacitor model. Greater thickness

Figure 4.3: Back-electret mic schematic

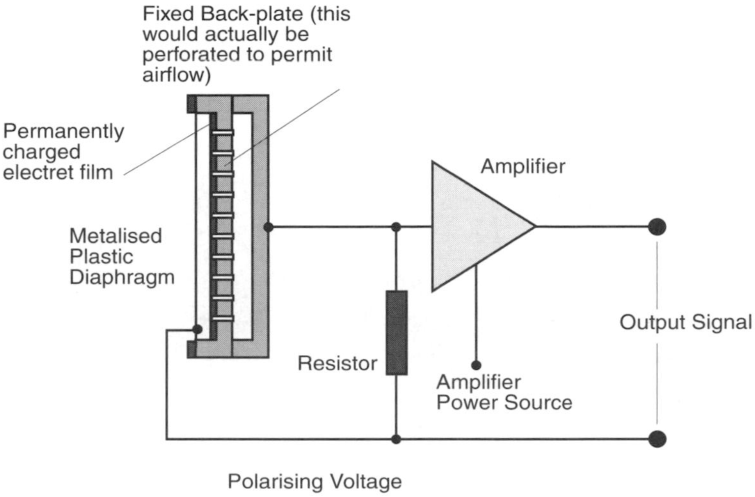
Fixed Back-plate (this would actually be perforated to permit airflow)
Permanently charged electret film
Metalised Plastic Diaphragm
Amplifier
Output Signal
Resistor
Amplifier Power Source
Polarising Voltage

means greater mass, and just as with the dynamic mic, that leads to poor sensitivity and a poor high frequency response.

back-electret mics

The performance of the electret mic improved dramatically when it was decided to try out a design where the permanently charged material was fixed to the capsule's stationary back-plate, allowing the same metalised plastic diaphragm to be used as on true capacitor models. The result was the back-electret microphone, and the best of these can rival a conventional capacitor microphone in all aspects of performance. In theory, the electrical charge on the capsule of an electret mic will leak away, but modern models are expected to remain stable for several decades. Figure 4.3 shows a back-electret microphone.

It's possible to buy a good back-electret mic for little more than a dynamic mic, yet they out-perform their dynamic counterparts by a significant margin in applications where sensitivity and high frequency response are important. Lower cost back-electret microphones often offer a choice of battery or phantom power operation, whereas better models operate

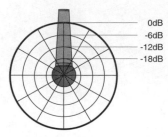

Omnidirectional:
This pattern picks up
sound equally in all
directions

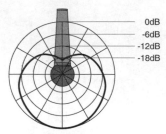

Cardioid:
Picks up sound
mainly from the front
and is least sensitive
at the rear

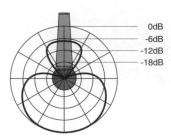

Hypercardioid:
Has a more tightly
focused frontal
pattern than the
cardioid, but is more
sensitive to sounds
coming directly from
behind. This pattern
is really half way
between the cardioid
and the
figure-of-eight

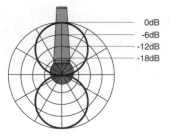

Figure-of-Eight:
This pattern picks up
sound both from the
front and rear, but not
from the sides

Figure 4.4: Common microphone patterns

from phantom power only as the increased voltage gives them more headroom.

cardioid mics

In the project or home studio where serious acoustic treatment is not usually an option, most recording is done using unidirectional pattern mics, so called because they pick up sound from mainly one direction. The common name for this type of microphone is the 'cardioid' which means heart-shaped. While the microphone may not be heart-shaped, the pickup pattern, if plotted on a circular graph is roughly heart-shaped. This shows the microphone is most effective when picking up sounds from in front, which helps to keep individual sounds separate and minimises the effect of room reflections.

proximity effect

The so-called proximity effect, which applies to cardioid pattern microphones (and also figure-of-eight models), results in a significant bass boost when the microphone is used with sound sources closer than a couple of centimetres. Used creatively, the proximity effect can give the experienced vocalist a means to add tone and expression to a performance, but in the studio, it is an unwelcome source of inconsistency.

omni mics

Omni mics, those that pick up sound equally well in all directions, are generally technically superior, but you run the risk of picking up unwanted sounds as well as the sounds you want. For example, where several instruments are playing in close proximity and each one has its own microphone, using omni microphones may allow too much unwanted sound leakage from one instrument into a mic intended for another instrument.

Some of the better capacitor mics have switchable polar patterns enabling them to work as Omni mics, cardioid mics or even figure-of-eight mics. The figure-of-eight pattern mic is equally sensitive both front and back, but the sides are completely dead. The figure-of-eight microphone is particularly useful in certain stereo recording applications. Figure 4.4 shows the three main polar patterns.

pzm microphone

The PZM or Pressure Zone Microphone, also known as a boundary microphone, is a special type of microphone where an omnidirectional

Figure 4.5: PZM mic

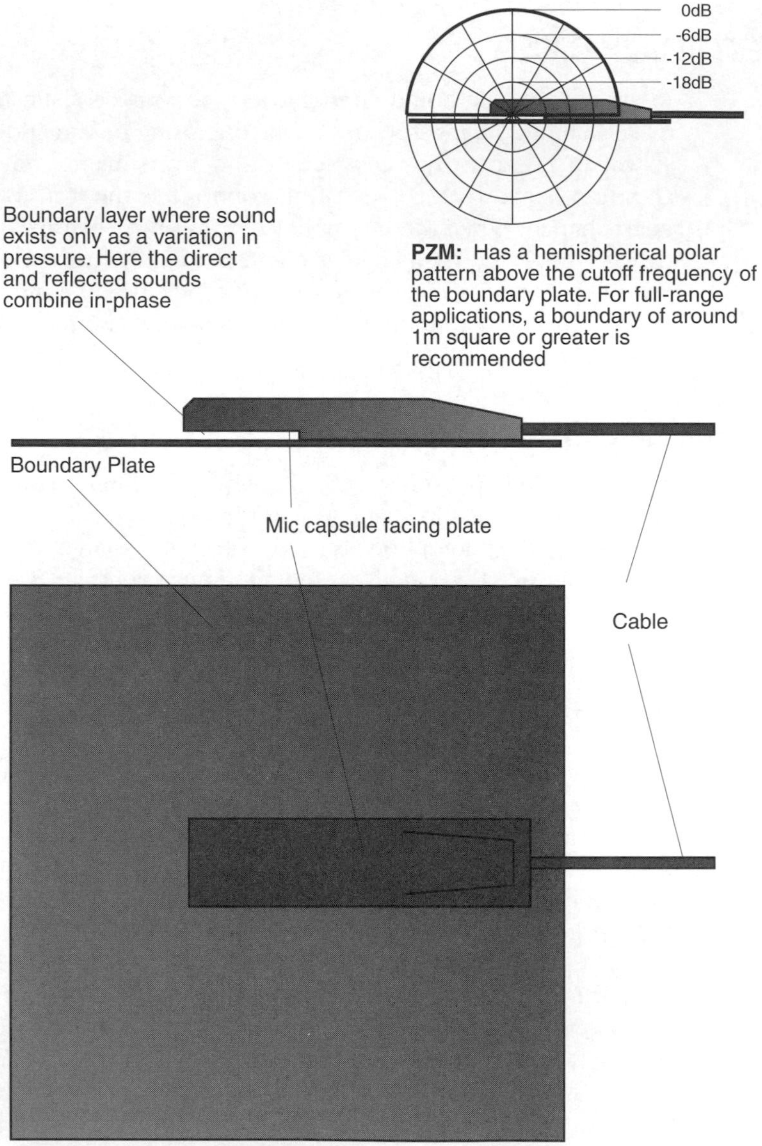
0dB
-6dB
-12dB
-18dB
Boundary layer where sound exists only as a variation in pressure. Here the direct and reflected sounds combine in-phase
PZM: Has a hemispherical polar pattern above the cutoff frequency of the boundary plate. For full-range applications, a boundary of around 1m square or greater is recommended
Boundary Plate
Mic capsule facing plate
Cable

capsule is suspended in close proximity to a reflective backplate or boundary. When a conventional microphone is placed within a room, it receives both direct and reflected sound, and because of phase differences caused by the longer path of the reflected sound, cancellation effects occur. The result is a so-called comb filtering effect where the frequency response of the combined direct and reflected sound shows a series of closely spaced peaks and troughs, rather like the teeth of a comb.

By placing the mic capsule very close to the boundary, the direct sound, and any sound reflected from the boundary, will arrive at the capsule at virtually the same instant, thus avoiding the comb filtering effect. Furthermore, because the reflected sound is essentially the same intensity as the direct sound, a doubling of output level occurs.

Because sound cannot be received from the other side of the boundary (the boundary itself is in the way), the polar pattern is confined to the hemispherical rather than the usual spherical pattern of the conventional omni microphone. However, for the boundary to reflect low frequencies effectively (and to enable it to reject low frequencies from the rear), the boundary size must be at least a quarter wavelength of the lowest frequency along each side. The boundary plate on which the capsule is mounted is far too small to be effective at low audio frequencies, so it is common practice to mount the microphone on either a rigid board measuring one metre square or more, or to place the microphone on a wall, floor or table top. If mounted on a table top, the microphone will pick up sound from all directions other than down, and by placing two PZM mics a metre or two apart, effective stereo recordings may be made. The main benefit of this type of microphone is its uncoloured sound due to the lack of undesirable comb filtering effects.

For a low cost introduction to this fascinating method of miking, try the Radio Shack/Tandy low cost PZM. This is an electret model and runs from batteries, so phantom power is not required, and PZM mics are suitable both for recording vocals and instruments. For budget vocal recording, try a low cost PZM mic taped to a mirror with a pop shield placed directly in front of it. A pop shield is simply a piece of fine gauze or mesh (nylon stocking material is best), designed to break up wind blasts from the singer's mouth.

mic characteristics

A theoretically perfect mic would have flat frequency response over the whole audio range, but this isn't always what we need. For example, some are designed with a deliberate degree of treble boost or presence to help vocals cut through a mix. Different models apply the treble boost in different parts of the spectrum, so it's important to choose a mic with characteristics that complement the singer.

Dynamic mics don't have as good a frequency response as capacitor mics, but they may be used in the studio because they deliver a more solid, hard-hitting vocal sound. They are also used for drum miking, electric and bass guitar miking and for some brass instruments. Dynamic mics with extended low frequency responses or pronounced bass boost characteristics are also built especially for kick drum miking.

Capacitor mics are the mics of choice for most vocal work and for most acoustic instruments. They're also used for stereo drum overheads as their good high frequency response lets them capture cymbal sounds with great accuracy. Good back-electret models may be used in the same way as capacitor models – the only practical difference is that back-electrets aren't built with switchable pickup patterns.

choosing a microphone

When choosing a microphone for a particular task, first determine whether the sound source is loud and close, or quiet and distant. If loud, you can choose either a dynamic microphone to give a solid, punchy sound or a capacitor microphone, which will produce a more transparent, detailed sound.

If the sound source is quiet or distant, then a capacitor microphone, or a back-electret, is the preferred choice because of its greater sensitivity. The directional characteristics of the microphone will depend on how close you can get to the sound source, how far away other sound sources are, and on the effect the room has on your sound. If several loud sources are close together, then a cardioid pattern microphone will help to reduce the spill, but in less difficult circumstances, an omni pattern microphone may produce a more natural sound.

Finally, should you choose a mic with a relatively flat frequency response or one with a presence peak? This is purely subjective, and particularly when working with vocalists, it is often best to try two or three different types of microphone to see which one suits the voice best. If the singer has a bright, sibilant voice, then a model with a strong presence peak might make this worse, but on the other hand, a voice lacking in definition will benefit from the extra brightness of a model with a presence peak. Making the best choice is all part of the engineer's skill and only comes with experience. Nevertheless, knowing what the important differences are between the different microphone types makes the choice much easier.

direct injection

Whenever you use a microphone, the result is dependent on both the quality of the microphone and on the acoustic character of the recording environment. All recording of actual sound must be done using a microphone, but many electronic musical instruments can be recorded using a method known as DI or Direct Injection. Direct Inject involves plugging a signal from an electronic or electric musical instrument into a recording system, often using some form of preamplifier or matching transformer rather than a traditional mic. DI recording techniques are suitable for bass and lead guitars (with suitable preamps), synths, samplers, drum machines and so on.

guitar di

Synths, samplers and drum machines can usually be connected directly to the line input of a mixer or multitracker, but because of their relatively high source impedance, guitars and basses have to be DI'd via a matching circuit of some kind. One solution is to use an active DI box, which matches the impedance of the guitar to that of the multitracker. These may be powered from batteries or from their mixer's own phantom power supply

While guitars and basses may be successfully DI'd using an active DI box, only clean sounds can be recorded in this way, because a guitar played through a guitar amplifier or combo is tonally coloured by the amplifier's circuitry and by the characteristics of the loudspeaker and its cabinet. To successfully record a convincing rock guitar sound, for example, it's best to use either a dedicated guitar recording preamp or go back to miking up your amp. Very often, miking a small practice amp will produce just as big a sound as a big stack. See the chapter on mic techniques for more information on recording various instruments.

speaker simulators

Any attempt to DI a guitar overdrive pedal will result in a rather thin and buzzy tone because you no longer have the guitar amp's circuitry or speaker to shape the sound. Most of the unwanted upper harmonics are filtered out by the restricted frequency response of a typical guitar loudspeaker. For this reason, recording guitar preamps include a piece of circuitry that functions as 'speaker emulator' by mimicking the frequency response of a guitar speaker. Separate speaker simulator boxes, both active and passive, are also available that can be used with pedals, the preamp output from a regular guitar amp or even the speaker output from a guitar amp.

chapter 5

equalisation

E qualisation can come in many forms, from the simple treble/bass control to the multi-band, parametric equaliser, but however you dress it up, equaliser is just another word for 'tone control'. The term equalisation came about because the very first equalisers were developed to help counteract or equalise other shortcomings in the system, but today, equalisation is often used creatively, and not just to fix problems. To understand EQ, it is necessary to understand a little about the audio spectrum as it relates to human hearing.

hearing range

Check any textbook on audio, and you'll see the limits of human hearing quoted as around 50Hz to 20kHz, though those very same books will also point out that very few individuals, other than young children, can hear pitches anything like as high as 20kHz. A more realistic figure might be around 15kHz for an adult, decreasing further as the years pass. What is really puzzling though, and this is scope enough for a book in its own right, is that even when your measured hearing response starts to fall off at way below 20kHz, it is still very easy to hear the effect of equalisation applied at the top end of the spectrum where you'd not expect to be able to hear the change. The plot thickens further when reputable studio engineers claim to be able to differentiate between two otherwise identical circuits, where one has been modified to handle frequencies up to 50kHz and one handles frequencies up to 30kHz. In theory, both limits are well above the limit of human perception, so it seems that what goes on outside the audible spectrum has a way of influencing what we perceive within the range of our own hearing systems.

You can try this for yourself by comparing a good capacitor mic (with an audio bandwidth in excess of 20kHz), with a dynamic microphone chosen to be nominally flat up to 15kHz or so, after which its response rolls off. Providing both have reasonably flat responses below their cut-off point, they should sound much the same to someone who is, in effect, deaf to all frequencies above 15kHz, but in practice, the high-frequency detail captured by the capacitor microphone lends it an entirely different character to the dynamic mic.

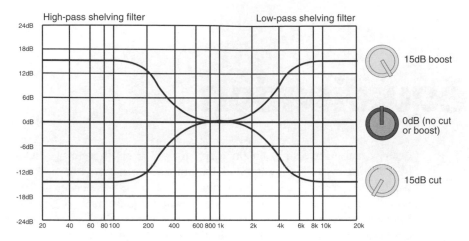

equaliser types

Though equalisers all do essentially the same job, there's a great deal of difference between a simple two-band treble/bass tone control and a multiband studio equaliser. The simplest equaliser is the shelving equaliser – a device that applies cut or boost, rather like a volume control, but only to the frequencies above or below the cut-off point of the equaliser, depending on whether the equaliser is based around a high-pass or a low-pass filter.

shelving filters

A low-pass shelving filter, as its name suggests, passes all frequencies below its cut-off frequency, but affects all frequencies above its cut-off frequency. Similarly, a high-pass filter passes all frequencies above its cut-off frequency, but affects all frequencies below its cut-off frequency. Figure 5.1 shows the frequency response graphs of a typical treble/bass EQ using high and low-pass filters. Note that the filter graph shows up as a slope at the cut-off point – it isn't possible, or desirable to have a filter that does nothing at one frequency, then, when you move up by just 1Hz, the filter comes in with full effect. Simple shelving filters typically have a 6dB per octave slope so that their influence is felt more progressively.

bandpass filters

A filter that passes frequencies between two limits is known as a bandpass filter, and if you have a mixer with a mid-range control, that will be a bandpass filter. On a typical mixer, the bandpass filter will have variable cut and boost, and it will be tunable so that its centre frequency can be varied.

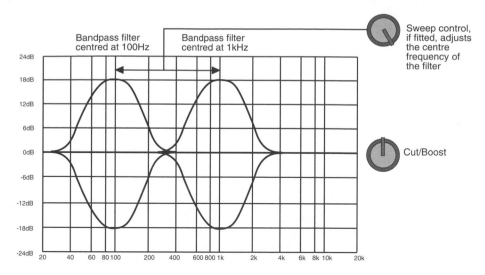

Figure 5.2: Bandpass filter response

This is known as a sweep equaliser, because although the filter frequency can be changed, the width of the filter cannot. Figure 5.2 shows a typical bandpass filter response.

parametric eq

A parametric EQ is very similar to a sweep bandpass EQ, except that a third control is added to allow the width of the filter to be adjusted. The width of a filter is sometimes described as its 'Q' value, where Q is the filter frequency divided by the number of Hz the filter affects. Because the filter response is curved, the actual frequency width is measured between the points on the graph where the signal level has fallen by 3dB. A high value for Q corresponds to a very narrow filter whereas a low value of Q corresponds to a wide filter. High Q values are useful for picking out sounds that occupy a very narrow part of the audio spectrum, whereas lower Qs produce a smoother, more musical sound.

A studio parametric EQ may have several filter sections so that three or four parts of the frequency spectrum can be treated simultaneously. Parametric EQs can be time consuming to set up properly, but they are the most powerful and most flexible of all EQ types. Figure 5.3 shows a typical parametric equaliser response.

graphic equaliser

A graphic equaliser can be recognised by a row of faders across the front panel, each fader controlling its own narrow section of the audio spectrum.

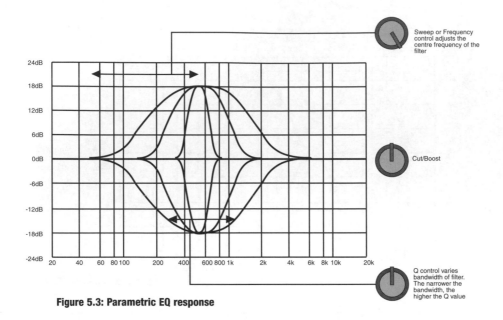

Figure 5.3: Parametric EQ response

For example, a 30-band graphic equaliser provides independent control over 30 different bands spaced one third of an octave apart.

Other than the highest and lowest faders, which control shelving filters, each of the filters in a graphic equaliser is a fixed frequency bandpass filter where boost is applied by moving the fader up from its centre position, and where cut is achieved by moving the fader down. Graphic equalisers have the advantage of being very easy to set up, but unless they are very well designed, they can have an adverse effect on the sound unless used sparingly. They are also less flexible than the parametric EQ, which can be exactly tuned to specific frequencies. With the graphic equaliser, the range covered by each fader is fixed, and the width of each individual band of a third octave equaliser is actually rather wider than a third of an octave so as to allow a smooth overlap between bands. Figure 5.4 shows the response of a typical graphic equaliser.

psychoacoustics of eq

Over the past couple of decades, EQ has moved further away from the corrective domain and, instead, has joined the more obvious effects boxes as a creative effect in its own right. Instead of simple bass and treble 'tone' controls, most recording mixers now offer additional mid-band control, often with a variable frequency or sweep function, and in more sophisticated systems, there's parametric EQ, which provides several bands of control where frequency, bandwidth and degree of cut/boost are all adjustable.

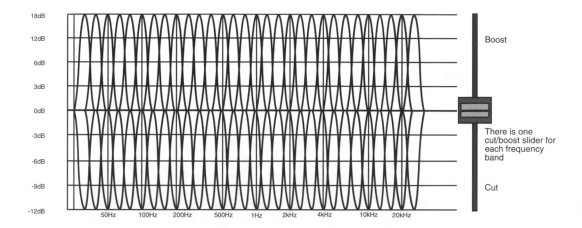

Figure 5.4: Graphic equaliser response

EQ and its perceived effect has much to do with psychoacoustics – the way that various nuances of sound affect our perception of the world around us. And, like so many areas of psychology, the root of psychoacoustics undoubtedly dates back to the days when survival was more important than setting up a really hot mix.

the effect of air

Nature has its own built-in EQ system in the form of distance. Low frequencies propagate slightly faster than high frequencies, so the further away the sound source is, the greater the lag between the fundamental pitch of a sound and its higher harmonics. Though this in itself doesn't change the spectral content of the sound, the change in the phase relationships of the various harmonics does cause us to perceive the sound as being more distant and, in terms of survival, less demanding of immediate attention.

The other thing that happens when a sound has to travel a long way is that the high frequencies are absorbed by frictional losses within the air itself and the higher the frequency, the greater the absorption. This does affect the spectral content of the sound and the further away a sound source is, the less bright it sounds. Again, less bright equates to more distant and less deserving of immediate attention, especially when closer sounds are being registered at the same time. In a real life setting, this might go along the lines of the howling wolves in the distant forest being less of a threat than

71

the sabre-toothed tiger dribbling and spitting six feet in front of you! In other words, nature's EQ is a means of making us pay attention.

Sabre-toothed tigers and wolves are not generally a problem in today's urban environment, but we still exhibit essentially the same instinctive reaction to sounds. It follows then that to get somebody's attention, you have to place a sound very close to them, and as recorded music is simply an illusion (stereo doubly so), you have to use the tools at your disposal to create the illusion of closeness. And that's what we're doing, often subconsciously, when we use EQ.

what does eq do?

Equaliser circuits are simply designed to lift or cut parts of the audio spectrum relative to other parts – think of EQ as a frequency selective volume control. But one of the side-effects of EQ is that the circuitry also introduces phase differences between the high and low frequency components of a signal. A touch of high frequency EQ and an increase in gain can make a distant sound appear closer by compensating for the high frequency loss due to air absorption, and at the same time, the phase changes introduced by the equaliser can help offset the fact that the higher harmonics have been delayed due to their passage through air. If adding high frequency EQ can make distant sounds appear to be closer, then it stands to reason that close-miked sounds can be made to appear even closer still by adding top end.

subjectivity

Why do different models of equaliser sound different, even though they claim to be working at the same frequency? While the effect of an equaliser's performance on the spectrum of the signal being processed is well documented, there's usually far less said about the way the equaliser affects the phase of the signal, and there's now a widely held belief that what an equaliser does to phase is just as important as what it does to frequency response. Indeed, some engineers believe that you can build an EQ that affects only phase, not the frequency spectrum, and in some respects, these opinions are given credence by the success of various enhancer circuits which have a minimal effect on the frequency spectrum of the sound being processed, yet create a significant impression of closeness and clarity. It's also true that a very small adjustment on a good equaliser will bring a sound out of a mix, while using a less sophisticated equaliser you might have to crank up the treble to a point where the signal sounds harsh and nasty before it achieves the required degree of 'up-frontness'.

audio cues

Audio is a complex subject, and there are non-EQ related audio cues to distance which also need to be simulated in order to create a convincing sense of distance or proximity. For example, if someone suddenly whispers in your ear, you hear far more direct sound than reverberant sound, whereas a distant sound may have a wide stereo spread and, depending on the environment, may contain a high proportion of reverberant information, especially in rocky or wooded areas.

the deep end

If high frequency EQ affects the apparent proximity of a sound by grabbing our attention, low frequency sounds seem to have a more subliminal effect, which is why repetitive, rhythmic sounds usually include a lot of low frequency information. You can have a really deep bass sound going on, which can add to the excitement of a track but without ever drawing your attention away from whichever sounds have been placed 'up front' in the mix. However, even the deepest sounds usually contain some high frequency harmonics so you can still use high frequency EQ to move these sounds forward in the mix if you want to make them demand attention.

perspective

If everything in a mix is close miked and given roughly the same EQ, then it's all going to try to push to the front where it will compete for our attention – and the human brain is noted for its intolerance of being asked to concentrate on too many different things at the same time. In a musical context, this leads to fatigue and a general sense of not wanting to listen any more. To check out what I mean, listen to a CD that's been recorded with everything too bright and you'll soon want it to 'get out of your face'. Intelligently used, EQ can place sounds in perspective with lead vocals and solos at the front, support instruments slightly behind, and sound effects at a distance. A mix is like a painting, and if all the colours are too bright, there'll be no way of differentiating between the foreground and the background.

spectral mixing

Most of the techniques discussed so far can be tried with just a simple bass/treble EQ, but if that's the case, why do we need mid-range controls or parametric equalisers? One obvious application of a bandpass filter, which is what mid-range and parametric equalisers are, is that you can 'tune, the equaliser to the fundamental pitch of an instrument and then add boost to increase the instruments' apparent level without having too much effect on sound either side. If the level of the instrument is then reduced by turning down the gain so as to restore the original subjective balance, frequencies produced by that instrument that are well away from the fundamental frequency will also be reduced in volume which helps reduce spectral overlap between sounds that might otherwise be too similar. To my mind, this is a corrective process rather than a creative one, and if you can choose more appropriate sounds at source you'll probably find that the end result is better than using EQ to 'bend' the sounds to fit. However, spectral mixing does work and it's worth exploring so you'll know its benefits and limitations.

loudness curve

One aspect of natural sound relates not to the sound itself but to the way the human hearing system works. While a good hi-fi amp has a perfectly flat frequency response, the human hearing system comes nowhere near to being flat. What's more, the frequency response changes depending on the level of the sound being heard. As a sound gets louder, we perceive more low end and more top end, but the mid-range becomes progressively more recessed. Looking at a frequency response graph, you'd see a curve with a dip in the centre, often known as a smile curve because of its obvious shape. The louder the sound, the deeper the smile. The loudness button on a stereo system emulates this smile curve so that you can play back material at a low volume level yet still get some impression of loudness.

In the studio, you can create a similar loudness effect by pulling down the mid EQ. Even physically quiet and distant sounds will appear louder – but they'll still seem far away. Pulling down the mid-range can also make a mix appear to be less cluttered, because a lot of the information that's clamouring for our attention resides in the upper mid-range. Using this knowledge, you could, for example, EQ an entire rhythm section to make it sound louder, then overlay this with conventionally EQ'd vocals and solo instruments. It's easy to make a mix sound loud by cranking up the monitors so that it is loud – but there's more skill in making a mix sound loud and powerful regardless of the playback level.

eq for positioning

I believe that there is value in listening to the various elements in a mix and then deciding on a 'pecking order' in terms of which sounds deserve the most attention and which ones play more of a supportive role. Then you can set up your EQ to help reinforce the natural sense of perspective. Most people try to achieve perspective using level control – everyone knows that the further away a sound is, the quieter it is – but now you know that you can also roll off a little top, just to consolidate the illusion.

eq cut

In most instances, the less EQ boost you use, the more natural the final sound will be, so rather than adding lots of top to vulnerable sounds such as vocals in order to get them to sit at the front of the mix, try being more restrained in your use of EQ and, instead, use high end cut on things like low-level pad sounds, backing vocals and whatever else is playing a subordinate role. This is particularly relevant to those who don't have access to really sweet-sounding, up-market EQs; most console EQs are a little unsubtle when used in anything but moderation.

No one approach will solve all your EQ problems – some difficult mixes are simply down to an unfortunate combination of instruments or sounds, or even plain bad arrangement. On the other hand, if you can get closer to the results you're after by using less EQ, then you just might break the unfortunate trend to mix fatiguing, over-bright records.

music and the spectrum

Having put forward an explanation for why I think equalisation works, it's time to look at the more common instruments used in pop music to see how EQ can be used to shape them. The first thing we need to know about an instrument is the range of frequencies it can produce, though if you don't have the figures written down, a little experimenting with EQ will soon tell you where the key elements of the sound reside.

The low-frequency limit of an instrument is usually defined as the fundamental frequency of its lowest note, but the high-frequency end is less easy to quantify. That's because nearly all musical sounds include harmonics that extend right to the top end of the audio spectrum and beyond, even though the level of these harmonics is probably very low.

bass instruments

Starting right at the bottom of the spectrum with bass sounds, the bass drum puts out most of its energy in a narrow band between 40Hz and 150Hz, depending on how it is tuned, but the attack transients reach right up into the upper mid-range. This can be confirmed by applying some EQ boost at around 4-6kHz; the difference in the attack characteristic is very noticeable.

The lowest note on the amplified electric bass guitar is 41Hz but the higher notes contain significant energy right up to 2 or 3kHz. Likewise, the traditional pipe organ goes an octave lower, down to 20Hz, where sounds are felt rather than heard. The organ's high notes may generate significant energy up at 8kHz and beyond.

The electric guitar has a starting point one octave higher than the bass guitar at 82Hz and, because of the restricted range of electric guitar speakers, there's little energy above 4kHz. Even so, it's a mistake to draw too many conclusions from the upper limit of any sound, because EQ applied above this arbitrary limit will almost certainly have some audible effect.

Moving a little higher up the spectrum, we find that vocals can range from around 80Hz to 1kHz, depending on the style and sex of the performer. Again, there's a significant amount of energy above that range, which is why live mic manufacturers often build in a presence peak at 3 or 4kHz.

Brass instruments also tend to occupy the mid-range of the spectrum, typically 80Hz to 1kHz, unless you count the tuba, in which case you can add almost an octave to the bottom of that figure. Few instruments produce the majority of energy at the high end of the spectrum, the piccolo and xylophone coming closest in the 600Hz to 5kHz range. The upper harmonics of cymbals, bell-trees, triangles and suchlike extend also well beyond the limit of human hearing. Sampled and synthesised sounds haven't been included, because they can cover whatever range the electrical circuitry is capable of supporting which, in theory, can be the entire audio spectrum.

reasons to eq

Some classical purists might say that you don't need EQ at all, but in the real world of pop recording, where the emphasis is on appropriate rather than accurate sounds, equalisation has become a way of life. After all, when was the last time you heard a pop record with a drum sound that bore any resemblance to an acoustic drum kit? Also, as explained earlier, EQ can be used to create or emphasise perspective within a mix.

This close miking of drums was originally devised to cut down on spill from other instruments, but the sound it produced (with some contribution from EQ), was so distinctive that it rapidly became the norm for pop records and the actual acoustic sound of the kit was largely forgotten.

In the case of the electric guitar, circumstance also dictated sound. During the pioneering days of electronics, amplifiers were pretty crude and tended to distort drastically at high volume levels. Likewise, speaker design wasn't really up to handling much power, and the brute-force twelve inch guitar speakers that became so popular couldn't reproduce any of the higher harmonics from guitar pickups. If modern technology had been available from the outset, electric guitars might have sounded as clean and bright as the acoustic guitar, but as it turned out, the combination of limited bandwidth speakers and excessive amounts of distortion led to the rock sound that we now take for granted.

Now that low distortion, high bandwidth digital sound processors are available, it's ironic that designers are all trying to write algorithms that successfully duplicate the sound of vintage guitar amplifiers. The reason I cite these examples is to show that equalisation can be used to shape familiar sounds in different ways – it isn't there just to fix problems caused by inappropriate recording techniques or equipment deficiencies.

separating sounds

EQ can be used creatively in many ways, but one of the most popular applications is to separate two similar sounds within a mix where the degree of overlap might cause the sound to become confused, or muddled. Some overlap is inevitable, but if, say, two electric guitars or a brass sample and string sample are fighting for the same space in a mix, EQ can often be used to reshape the sounds, forcing them into slightly narrower areas of the spectrum.

For example, a peaking equaliser can be used to add a degree of bite to one sound at one frequency while the other sound can be peaked up at a different frequency. Similarly, the top or bottom end of a sound can be 'trimmed' to avoid conflict, a typical example being the acoustic rhythm guitar in a pop mix, where it is common practice to filter out the bottom end quite drastically. This leaves a bright guitar sound that sits well in the mix but without the bassy, boxy element that might overlap with the other mid-range instruments or the vocals.

At this point, it is valuable to examine a few common instruments to see how EQ can be used most effectively.

bass guitar

During the sixties, the bass guitar was used to provide little more than a low-frequency pulse; its sound was invariably dull by comparison with today's bass sounds. The contemporary bass guitar sound, by contrast, is partly a result of changing from tape-wound to wire-wound strings, of new playing styles, and of the degree of equalisation that can be applied using a modern bass guitar amplification system.

Boosting at around 80Hz can pull out the low bass, while boosting between 500Hz and 800Hz adds a nicely aggressive bite. Boosting higher up the spectrum tends to bring out the finger noise and little else, so if a bright sound is what you're after, get it as close as you can to what you want before you add EQ. Playing technique has a lot to do with the tone of a bass guitar and no amount of EQ will compensate for a feeble finger-style of playing.

A touch of low-mid cut at around 200-250Hz can sometimes be effective in combination with a little low-end boost; this warms up the low bass end without allowing the low-mid area to get uncontrollably boomy.

bass synth sounds

Bass synths can be treated in much the same way, though their ability to produce higher harmonics means that EQ at higher frequencies will also be effective. However, be cautious when using very bright bass synth sounds; they can so easily fill up all the space in a mix, leaving the whole thing sounding congested.

electric guitar shaping

The electric guitar is not a natural instrument, so anything you want to do to it using EQ is okay if it works on an artistic level. If you need to add warmth to the sound of an electric guitar, concentrate on the area between 125Hz and 200Hz. There's no point adding boost much below this region, as the lowest note's fundamental frequency is 82Hz. Bass boost will only bring up the cabinet boom and make the overall sound muddy; it could also conflict with the bass guitar. Equally important, boosting the bass end will accentuate any mains hum in the signal – most guitar pickups, especially single-coil versions, pick up a surprising amount of hum.

To add attack to the sound, go for the 2-4kHz region of the spectrum, but don't add any really high-end boost unless the guitar is DI'd, as there's not much coming out of a guitar speaker above 3 or 4kHz. All you'll do is bring up the background noise and, if the guitar is being used with an overdrive sound, this will tend to go buzzy or fizzy.

In a congested mix, two similar-sounding electric guitars can be separated by adding bite at different frequencies, say one guitar at 3kHz and one at 4kHz. However, this is rarely as successful as getting a different sound at source. If you can use two different amplifiers or preamp settings while recording the two parts it will help. It also makes sense to use different types of guitar – perhaps one with single-coil pickups and one with humbuckers. If you're miking the guitar amp, try using different mics for the different parts – a dynamic for one take and a capacitor for the other will make a noticeable difference, even if the guitar, amp and player remain the same.

I try to record acoustic guitars with as little EQ as possible, preferring to move the mics in order to get the right basic tone. But players and producers always seem to want to add more top end, so some EQ is inevitable. More severe EQ may be called for if the acoustic guitar is playing rhythm in a pop mix, because the body resonance can clash with the other instruments in the arrangement. To thin the sound out a little, try cutting below 200Hz. Boosting in the region of 4 to 6kHz adds a nice American jangle, but you need a good guitar with fresh strings to really make this work. You also need to use a good-quality capacitor microphone, as dynamic mics are insufficiently sensitive and fail to reproduce the high-frequency detail which characterises a good acoustic guitar sound.

vocals

When recording vocals, always use a pop shield, as no amount of EQ will fix popping once it's on tape. General brightening can be achieved using the shelving high EQ control on the mixer, but keep a wary ear open for sibilance. Boosting lower down, at 1-2kHz, gives a rather honky, cheap sound to the vocals and so is not recommended other than as a special effect. Presence can be added by boosting gently at 3-4kHz using the upper mid sweep equaliser, but be sparing in this as the natural character of the voice can easily be lost. In a mix of backing vocals, rolling off a touch of bass often helps the sound fit in better with the mix.

drums

Drums are a special case when it comes to equalisation, because the accepted pop and rock drum sound is not that of a natural kit. The trick is to make the drums sound both bright and solid but not too 'thick'.

kick drum

A close-miked bass drum or kick drum without EQ will often sound less than ideal, though you may strike it lucky. Most often there is a need to add definition to the hit, plus a degree of low-frequency weight. For a straightforward, punchy sound, a little boost at 80Hz will almost always improve matters, but to get a deeper sound without the end result being either boomy or too stodgy, try adding 10dB or so of boost with your shelving bass control (most consoles have their bass controls at 50 or 60Hz) and then wind in 10dB or so of cut at around 220Hz using the lower mid control. The two controls work together to produce a narrow area of low-frequency boost rather than the rather wide, uncontrollable boost that is obtained by using the low EQ on its own.

To add definition to the beater impact, boost the upper mid-range between 3 and 6kHz, choosing the final setting by ear. A wooden beater is far better than a felt one for producing a modern kick drum sound, and the slap can be further enhanced by taping a piece of thin plastic (for example, a piece of credit card), on the drum head at exactly the spot where the beater impacts.

toms

Toms may be handled in much the same way as bass drums, with boost in the 80 to 120Hz region adding punch and depth. Careful adjustment of the upper mid control can help pick out the stick impact, and if the tom rings on too much or if it rings in sympathy with other drums, you can usually afford to roll off quite a lot of low bass without the result sounding thin in the context of a mix.

snare drums

Snare drums are quite unpredictable and you never quite know how they're going to sound until you've put up a mic and listened to the result over the monitors. The sound can be fattened by boosting the 90-140Hz band, while the bite can usually be located in the 3-7kHz region. It's easiest, when searching for the right area, to apply full boost then tune for the appropriate pitch. Once you've found it, you can back off the degree of boost until you have a sound you can live with. If the drum still doesn't sound crisp enough, consider switching to a capacitor mic.

cymbals

Always record cymbals at a low level to prevent tape overload and keep in mind that they always cut through more loudly than you expect. Brightness can be added using the shelving high EQ control or you can tune the upper mid control until you find a sweet spot. In general, cymbals are recorded as part of the overhead mic mix and, in some cases, it can help to roll off the bass end quite significantly to prevent the drum sounds picked up by the overheads from obstructing the drum sounds from the close mics.

strings and brass

Relatively few home studio owners get a chance to work with live brass or string players, but the high quality sound that comes from a modern sample library patch can be EQ'd in much the same way as the real thing. Brass and string instruments work on entirely different principles, but they do respond to equalisation in similar ways. Between 1kHz and 3.5kHz the sound can become nasal or honky, which means a little subtle cutting in this region can sweeten things up. To add high-end sizzle, move up to the 6-10kHz band and try a little boost there, but don't overdo it or the sound will become 'spitty'. For a warm pad sound from string or brass samples and synth patches, roll off a little top and add a hint of boost between 300 and 400Hz.

piano

To record a real piano you'll need a pair of good mics, but again, you can apply the following suggestions to piano samples if they're not already to your liking. The bass end can be warmed up by gently boosting at 90-150Hz, while the attack detail can be brought out by bringing up the 4-6kHz section of the spectrum. If the sound is boomy, look for the offending area between 250 and 350Hz and apply just enough cut to keep it under control.

Because the piano is such a natural and familiar instrument, it pays to use less EQ and concentrate instead on putting suitable mics in the right place. Electronic pianos can be equalised in the same way, though many models offer such a range of piano sounds that equalisation may be quite unnecessary.

overview

Equalisation should always be brought into play after you've done your best to get the right sound at source, and there's a huge subjective difference in sound between a budget equaliser and a top quality studio equaliser. Though difficult to quantify, really good equalisers allow you to make more drastic changes without the sound appearing unnatural.

It is also important to understand that the human ear is far less critical of EQ cut than it is of boost, so if you can solve the problem by cutting the area of the spectrum that seems to be too loud, the result will be more natural. Often a combination of cut and boost is required, but always use the bypass switch to flip back and forth between the equalised and unequalised sounds, to make sure you really have improved matters. Equally, when you have EQ'd an instrument in isolation, make sure that the setting you have chosen works in context with the rest of the mix, as parts invariably sound quite different once everything else is playing.

If you strive to get your sounds right at the outset, EQ is an invaluable ally in shaping those sounds to your liking, but don't make the mistake of thinking that EQ can be used to salvage poor work.

chapter 6

setting up a home studio

To the uninitiated, a home studio is a bewildering jumble of speakers, cables, boxes and winking LEDs, but no matter how complicated the system, the essential components are roughly the same. You have to have a source of sound to record, such as the output from a microphone, you have to have a machine upon which to record, and you need some form of loudspeaker and amplifier system to play back your work. At its simplest, you could make recordings with just a stereo cassette deck, a pair of headphones and a couple of electret microphones, but I'm assuming that most people reading this book will either have (or aspire to), a 4-track, cassette-based system or a separate multitrack tape recorder and mixer. It's also possible to set up a combined MIDI and audio studio using a simple mixer, a PC computer and a suitable soundcard, but that particular avenue will be explored in a separate chapter.

the components

In a commercial recording studio, the nerve centre of the studio is the mixing console, but if you have a cassette Multitracker, Portastudio or one of the Minidisc or hard disk-based integrated multitrackers, the mixer and multitrack recorder are combined in a single piece of hardware. This not only saves space, but also cuts down the amount of wiring required. It also sidesteps any potential matching problems between the recorder and mixer. The terms Multitracker and Portastudio are registered trademarks of Fostex and Tascam respectively, so I'll use the term multitracker with a lower case 'm' to describe a generic combined multitrack recorder and mixer.

what else do you need?

You could just plug a microphone or two into your multitracker, put on a pair of headphones and start recording, but unless you're going to work at a very basic level, you're going to need some other hardware to go with it.

The first extra you're definitely going to need is a stereo tape machine on which to mix your finished recordings, and the better the machine, the better the quality of your final recording. A good cassette deck will give acceptable results for demo work, but if you want to try for more professional quality results, then choose a DAT digital recorder. These are rather more expensive than hi-fi cassette decks, but they can record at true CD (16-bit) quality.

Almost as good as DAT, but rather cheaper, are the new DCC machines, originally intended for the consumer marketplace. Technically, the sound quality isn't as good as DAT because data compression is used to squeeze a lot of information onto a relatively small amount of tape, but in practice, few people can tell the difference, especially on pop music. Certainly the side-effects of data compression are insignificant compared to the side effects of the analogue tape noise reduction systems used on semi-pro multitrack and domestic stereo tape machines. Sony's Minidisc system is also a possibility for home mastering, though it tends to cost rather more than DCC. On the plus side, Minidisc offers instant access to recorded material, much like a conventional CD player.

Other stereo mastering options are to use the sound tracks of a hi-fi video recorder or to buy an open reel stereo recorder such as a used Revox or Tascam 32. Open reel mastering machines have the advantage that you can edit your recordings using a razor blade and splicing tape. They also produce far better recordings than analogue cassette machines.

Whatever mastering format you choose to mix down to, the machine is known as a master recorder and the stereo mixes you produce are called master tapes. It is from these master tapes that any subsequent copies (or records and CDs), are made.

the monitoring system

It's never a great idea to do all your recording and mixing on headphones as they often give quite a different impression to loudspeakers, especially when you're trying to evaluate bass sounds. Ideally, you should check your work on both headphones and speakers For home use, a stereo hi-fi amp of at least 30 watts per channel is recommended along with a pair of accurate loudspeakers. Ensure your hi-fi amplifier has either Aux, CD or Tuner inputs; you can plug your multitracker's stereo monitor output into any of these. However, you can't use the Phono record deck inputs as these have built-in tonal correction for record decks.

loudspeakers

No matter how sophisticated your studio, everything you do will eventually be judged by what comes out of your monitor loudspeakers. Choose the most honest-sounding speakers you can find, even if they don't sound the most impressive. Medium size two-way hi-fi speaker systems are usually fine for home recording, though dedicated near-field monitors tend to be more resistant to abuse. Whatever speakers you choose, try to listen to a selection of well-recorded CDs over them so that you get familiar with the sound. That way your mixes are likely to be more accurate, making it more likely that they'll also sound good on other hi-fi systems. It also pays to double-check your mixes on a cheap system such as a ghetto blaster or a car stereo system.

microphones

You're going to need at least one microphone to record vocals and acoustic instruments, and most studio set-ups will need more than one, especially if two or more performers want to record at the same time. Choosing the right microphone can be confusing, so check out the chapter on microphone types so that you know how the various types differ. If you already have a decent dynamic live vocal mic, it should handle most jobs adequately, though a capacitor microphone is better for recording quieter acoustic instruments.

You should also read your multitrack workstation manual before buying a mic to see whether you need to use high or low impedance mics. All professional mics are low impedance and balanced, though they can be used unbalanced with a suitable lead. If the mic has an XLR connector built into the handle and comes with a separate lead, then it's almost certainly low impedance and balanced.

Capacitor mics require 48V phantom power and few multitrack workstations provide this. If you want to use one of these mics, you'll need an external mic preamp with its own phantom power source. A more cost-effective solution is to choose a good back-electret mic that can be operated from an internal battery.

effects

Modern recordings make extensive use of electronic effects, even though this may not be obvious from listening to the record. The most useful effect is without doubt the reverb processor, but most of today's effects units provide a whole range of different effects for you to use. These are

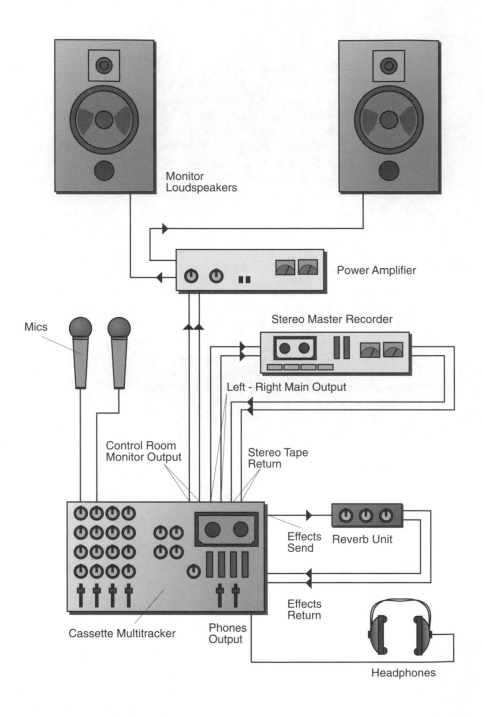

Monitor
Loudspeakers

Power Amplifier

Stereo Master Recorder

Left - Right Main Output

Mics

Control Room
Monitor Output

Stereo Tape
Return

Effects
Send

Reverb Unit

Effects
Return

Cassette Multitracker

Phones
Output

Headphones

Figure 6.1: Recording system connections

commonly known as multieffects units and there's a full chapter on effects later in the book. At a minimum, you'll need one stereo reverb unit, but the ideal situation is to have at least one good reverb unit and one multieffects unit. Refer to the chapter on effects for more details of what the various effects do and how to connect them.

the system

Figure 6.1 shows how the various parts of a home recording system based around an integrated multitracker are connected. If you're using a hi-fi system to provide monitoring, the amplifier should be switched to Aux when recording and overdubbing, and to Tape when you want to hear your stereo mixes played back from the mastering machine. All cables should be kept as short as possible.

When setting up your studio, everything should be within reach and the speakers should be positioned symmetrically about the listening position. However, don't place speakers too close to corners or the bass response will change unpredictably.

facilities

Studio effects can be very flexible, but you'll need a multitrack workstation equipped with effects send and return facilities to make full use of them. Fortunately, all but the very cheapest 'musical notepad' type multitrackers have aux sends and returns. If the term 'aux' is unfamiliar to you, refer back to the chapter on mixers. Modern digital effects units have stereo outputs, so a multitrack workstation with at least one stereo aux return or two spare Input channels is required.

The other important signal processor that it's hard to live without is the compressor. A compressor is basically a type of automatic level control that tries to smooth out the differences between loud and quiet sounds, and most vocal tracks benefit from compression to keep them sounding even. If you intend to use a compressor, you'll need a multitracker with insert points on at least some of the channels. An insert point is a socket that lets you patch an external processor 'in-line' with the signal passing through the mixer channel.

You can't plug a mic directly into a typical compressor (or any other signal processor for that matter) as they are normally designed for line-level operation only. However, so-called voice channels are available where a mic amp is combined with a compressor and sometimes an equaliser. These may be used to treat a mic signal directly, and purists often prefer to plug these directly into the multitrack recorder, thus bypassing the mixer altogether. This may or may not be possible on a multitracker, depending on the facilities available, but where it is possible, it usually results in a noticeable improvement in sound quality.

headphones

Though I've already pointed out that headphones are not great for critical mixing without at least double-checking your mixes on loudspeakers, they are useful for working at times when making excessive noise would be antisocial, and they're absolutely essential for performer monitoring while overdubbing. Don't skimp on headphones, even a really good pair will cost significantly less than a decent pair of nearfield monitor speakers.

open phones

Open or semi-enclosed hi-fi headphones usually sound most natural but they tend to be bass light compared to fully enclosed phones. High quality headphones are particularly useful for checking stereo positioning and for showing up noises or distortion that you might miss when listening over loudspeakers. Providing you check your mix over loudspeakers at critical points, headphones can allow you to work at night when you might otherwise have to stop because of noise constraints. Open phones are probably the nicest to work with, though you'll need to ask your speakers for a second opinion concerning the bass end of your mix.

enclosed phones

For monitoring while overdubbing, enclosed headphones are preferred because they don't allow much sound to leak in or out. Some of the better enclosed headphones are accurate enough for checking mixes, so if your budget only stretches to one pair of phones, a good enclosed pair might be the best option. However, try out as many pairs as you can and see how the sound compares with what you hear over loudspeakers. Check your multitrack workstation manual to see what impedance of headphone it can drive.

system connections

Most of the signal connections in a typical home studio are made using regular instrument jack leads or RCA phono hi-fi cables. Only microphones require special cables, though which ones you need depends on the input connectors of your mixer or multitracker. Very basic models may have inputs on jacks, whereas more serious models will have balanced XLR inputs. The multitrack workstation and cassette deck usually connect to the hi-fi power amplifier by means of standard RCA phono leads, though more professional amplifiers have balanced inputs on XLR connectors or balanced jacks

Speakers should be connected using heavy, twin cable, not instrument coax leads. Keep the speaker cables as short as possible and make them the same length. There's no need to buy expensive speaker cable – what matters most is that it is thick enough to have a very low electrical resistance. Inadequate speaker cable will not only cause a loss of volume, but the sound will also be compromised.

Setting up a system using a separate mixer and multitrack recorders isn't much more complicated, but you do need a bunch of cables to carry the mixer's group outputs to the multitrack machine's inputs, and another bunch of cables to link the multitrack's output to the mixer's tape inputs. All signal cables between the mixer and multitrack recorder must be screened.

mains wiring

In a typical studio, there are lots of mains-powered boxes, but mains wiring should be kept as far away from the signal wiring as is practical, and if possible, mains and signal leads should cross at right angles to reduce the amount of interference picked up from the 50 or 60Hz mains. The worst situation for interference is where mains and signal cables run close alongside each other for any distance. Here the signal cable tends to act as an aerial and picks up the hum radiated by the mains cable.

Don't remove the earth leads from any equipment that's supposed to be earthed and check your mains plugs regularly; loose wires are not only dangerous but will also cause intermittent crackles and buzzes. The use of multiway connector blocks is inevitable in the small studio – mine contains dozens of the things, but avoid plugging leads in and out of them too often as the socket spring tends to go slack eventually, and that can result in bad contacts.

studio layout

As touched upon very briefly earlier on, you should set up your equipment so that it's easy to reach when in use. In the larger studio, it may not be possible to reach everything, but you should at least be able

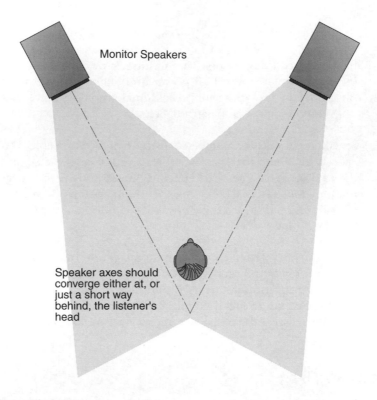

Monitor Speakers

Speaker axes should
converge either at, or
just a short way
behind, the listener's
head

Figure 6.2: Monitor positioning

to get your hands on the controls you use most often. If you play keyboards or have a MIDI sequencer, you'll also need to think about where these go.

speaker placement

It's important to have the speakers set up symmetrically and in front of you, otherwise your stereo image will be affected; when using small speakers in a home studio, it's usually best to have them around one metre away and about the same distance apart as shown in Figure 6.2. It's also advisable to keep the speakers at least half a metre away from corners; putting speakers close to corners causes an artificial increase in bass which may affect the way you mix. Backing speakers right up against a wall may also cause an artificial increase in bass response. In a rectangular room, it's usually best to position the speakers along the longest wall.

While it's quite common to see speakers standing on a shelf, table or on top of a mixing console, acoustically, it's better if the speakers are on stands behind your equipment desk or mixer as this cuts down on unwanted, reflected sound. It's also better to mount the speakers upright rather than to lay them on their sides; keeping them upright will produce a wider listening area within which the mix sounds accurate. The optimum listening position is exactly between the speakers and is sometimes called the 'sweet spot'. To ensure the sweet spot is as wide as possible, the speakers should be angled so the tweeters point either at or just behind the listener's head; the tweeters should be at head height or the speakers angled to point at the engineer's head.

acoustic treatment

Professional recording studios are designed to include elaborate acoustic treatment, but in the home studio, there's usually insufficient budget and space to add anything but very simple acoustic treatment. When mixing, most problems are caused by loud reflections from the walls, floors and ceilings of a room, which all confuse the direct sound of the speakers. From this, you might rightly deduce that cutting down on excessive reflections is an obvious move, though you don't want to deaden your room so much that it sounds as though you're in a padded cell. Ordinary carpets, curtains and soft furnishings help enormously, and if you can hang heavy rugs or drapes on the rear wall, facing the speakers, this will deaden the sound even more.

It's important not to try too hard to absorb too much reflected sound because bass frequencies tend not to be absorbed as much as high frequencies. If you do add too much absorbent material, the room is likely to sound dull and bassy, so aim for something like the acoustics of a domestic living room rather than something that sounds completely dead. In a typical carpeted room, little extra treatment should be necessary. One of the benefits of nearfield monitoring is that, because the speakers are physically close, you hear more of the direct sound from the speakers and less of the reflected sound from the room, making room acoustics less of an issue. Also relevant is the fact the nearfield monitors don't produce a lot of deep bass, and though heavy bass might sound impressive, unless the control room is acoustically treated, the bass you hear is likely to be very misleading. Far better to have an accurate sound with less bass.

If the room is excessively reverberant, try hanging a rug (or thick drape) on the rear wall and two smaller ones on the side walls either side of your normal listening position. If you can hang the rugs around 30mm from the walls, they will be more effective than if they are fixed directly to the walls. Foam acoustic tiles or slabs of two inch, fireproof furniture foam are also

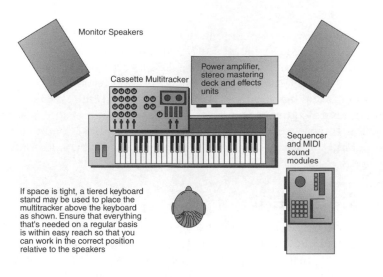

Monitor Speakers

Cassette Multitracker

Power amplifier, stereo mastering deck and effects units

Sequencer and MIDI sound modules

If space is tight, a tiered keyboard stand may be used to place the multitracker above the keyboard as shown. Ensure that everything that's needed on a regular basis is within easy reach so that you can work in the correct position relative to the speakers

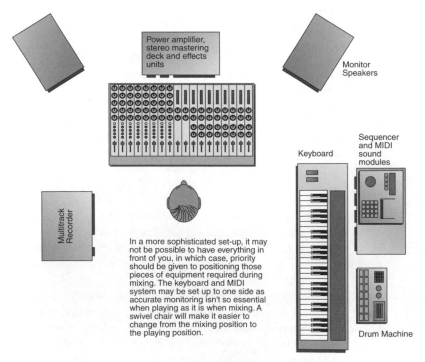

Power amplifier, stereo mastering deck and effects units

Monitor Speakers

Sequencer and MIDI sound modules

Keyboard

Multitrack Recorder

In a more sophisticated set-up, it may not be possible to have everything in front of you, in which case, priority should be given to positioning those pieces of equipment required during mixing. The keyboard and MIDI system may be set up to one side as accurate monitoring isn't so essential when playing as it is when mixing. A swivel chair will make it easier to change from the mixing position to the playing position.

Drum Machine

Figure 6.3: System layout example

setting up a home studio

very effective at mid and high frequencies. Bedroom studios often work well with little or no extra treatment because the carpets, curtains and bed are very effective at absorbing sound.

It should be noted that acoustic treatment is not the same thing as soundproofing. Hanging acoustic tiles around the walls, or sticking egg boxes everywhere may change the acoustics of the room, but it will do little to prevent unwanted sound leaking in or out.

Figure 6.3 shows a possible studio layout incorporating a MIDI keyboard and sequencer. The position of additional absorbent material is indicated. Where a separate mixer and multitrack recorder are used, the layout is similar with the mixer being at the centre of the action, though it may be more convenient to move the recorder to one side or the other.

patchbays

Patchbays often look daunting, but their sole purpose is to bring some degree of order to the potential wiring chaos of the recording studio. While many of the connections in a typical studio can be left alone, many more need to be changed on a daily basis. For example, you may have a compressor that needs to be patched into different mixer insert points as required, or you may want to move an effects unit from one send to another. Then there are those occasions when you need to copy a DAT tape, perhaps via an equaliser and enhancer onto cassette, but later in the day, you might need the enhancer to process a stereo subgroup on your mixer or the equaliser to process a couple of input channels. No matter how you try to rationalise your system, you never seem to get away without having to repatch things.

Rewiring in a system without patchbays is awkward, mainly because most bits of studio gear have their connections at the back where you can't get at them easily. Similarly, mixer insert points may or may not be easily accessible, depending on the make and model, but most use stereo jacks, so unless you have an endless supply of Y leads or adaptors, they're not easy to use, even if you can get to them.

A properly thought out patchbay brings all your regularly used audio connections out to a single patch panel, enabling you to make any necessary connections by plugging in short patch cables. However, it rarely makes sense to bring absolutely everything out to a patchbay, because there are some things you may never need to change. For example, if you have more effects sends and returns than you have effects units, you could leave your effects permanently wired to the console rather than use a patchbay. If you have any spare console sends and returns, you could then bring these out to the patchbay to enable you to patch in effects which clients or friends might bring round.

jack bays

At its simplest, a patchbay can be thought of as a system of extension cables that brings the necessary input and output points to an easily accessible panel. Most semi-pro studios use standard jack patchbays, because they are relatively inexpensive, and because they interface easily with most musical and hi-fi equipment such as synths, effects, pedals, guitar preamps, cassette decks and so on.

The most common form of jack patchbay uses standard jacks both for patching and for rear panel connections, which means you can wire up all your system using conventional jack leads, making it easy to reconfigure your patchbay when you want to integrate a new piece of equipment. So called 'hard wired' patchbays where the rear connections are soldered directly to your cable harness are cheaper and arguably more reliable, but changing things later is less straightforward. Currently, the most popular type of jack patchbay fits a 1U panel and has two rows of 24 sockets. Convention dictates that the lower sockets are inputs and the top row are outputs.

Where a patchbay is used to provide access to the ins and outs of effects processors, to the input channels of a mixer and so on, a basic non-normalised patchbay is required. In other words, the socket at the back of the patchbay connects directly to the socket on the front and nowhere else. Such a connection system is called non-normalised – the sockets are purely extensions of whatever the patchbay is connected to.

normalising

In the case of insert points, we need another type of patchbay where the upper and lower sockets are connected by means of so-called normalising contacts when no patch plugs are inserted. The reason for this is related to the way in which console insert points are wired. Usually there's a stereo TRS insert jack socket on the console, which includes a pair of switch contacts so that the insert send is connected directly to the insert return if no jack is inserted. If this were not the case, there would be no continuous signal path through the mixer channel unless a processor of some type was plugged into the insert point. The chapter on mixers explains insert points more fully.

Once you connect a patchbay to a mixer insert point, the mixer's internal signal path is broken because now there's a jack permanently plugged into the mixer insert socket. If we didn't do something about this, it would mean that whenever you didn't have a processor plugged into the patchbay, you'd have to use a patch cable to join the top and bottom sockets simply to complete the circuit. This would need a lot of patch leads and would make for a very congested patchbay, so instead, we use so-called normalised patchbays with internal switch contacts to do this for us automatically. When no connection is made to the patchbay, the input jack is connected directly to the output jack.

semi normal

In some circumstances, it can be useful to take a signal from an insert send without breaking the signal path. For example, you might want to split a signal so that you can feed it both through the mixer channel and into a signal processor at the same time. To make this easy, the semi-normalised patchbay was developed; when nothing is plugged in, the patchbay output (insert send) is connected back to its input (insert return) via the normalising contacts. However, by fitting normalising contacts only to the lower (input socket), whenever a jack is plugged into the output socket only, the input still remains connected to the output and the signal flow is not interrupted. Conversely, whenever a jack is plugged into the input (lower socket), the signal path is broken. By using this type of patchbay, you can plug into the top socket on its own to split the signal, or you can plug into both to connect a signal processor to the console's insert point.

The term 'sniff and break' is sometimes used to describe this type of patchbay; plugging into the patchbay output socket allows you to 'sniff' the signal without affecting the existing signal flow, while plugging into the patchbay input breaks the signal flow. Semi-normalised 'sniff and break' operation is now almost universal, even when the patchbay is said to be normalised, and there's no obvious advantage in a fully normalised patchbay connection scheme. Most commercial patchbays include some form of link or other simple switching system to allow them to be configured for either semi-normalised or non-normalised operation. Figure 6.4 shows how both non-normalised and semi-normalised patchbays are wired, and if you only need a few patch points, you could copy this wiring arrangement to build your own.

balancing?

Most home studios use unbalanced patching systems simply because

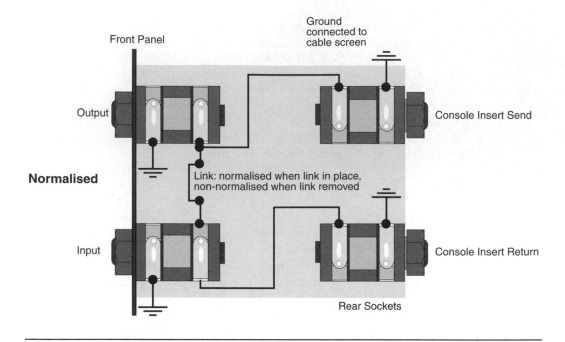

Front Panel

Ground connected to cable screen

Output — Console Insert Send

Normalised

Link: normalised when link in place, non-normalised when link removed

Input — Console Insert Return

Rear Sockets

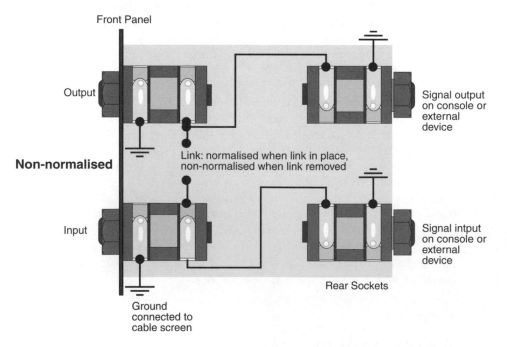

Front Panel

Output — Signal output on console or external device

Non-normalised

Link: normalised when link in place, non-normalised when link removed

Input — Signal intput on console or external device

Rear Sockets

Ground connected to cable screen

Figure 6.4: Semi-normalised patchbay

most synths and preamps have unbalanced outputs. Insert points are also unbalanced on all but the very top end pro studio consoles. However, if you want to use a patchbay to provide access points between the balanced outputs of a mixer and the balanced inputs of a multitrack recorder, it is probably worth using a balanced patchbay for this application. This will require stereo jack patch leads, though most systems will allow you to use unbalanced mono jacks to feed unbalanced signals into a balanced input.

what to connect

It's always a good idea to bring out all your console insert points to a semi-normalised patchbay, including the group inserts and the master (stereo output) inserts. If you don't want to wire up all the channel inserts, then decide which channels you are likely to use for microphones and take their inserts to the patchbay so you can patch in compressors when recording.

In more sophisticated systems, it may be useful to connect a normalised patchbay between your mixer group outs and the multitrack inputs allowing you, for example, to route a DI box or mic preamp directly to tape without having to pass the signal through the mixer. Similarly, you might want to use a semi-normalised patchbay to bring the multitrack returns back into the line inputs of the mixer, especially if your console has no Line/Tape switch.

As stated earlier, non-normalised patchbays are simple extension leads and are useful for bringing out the console line inputs, effects sends and effects returns, and channel direct outputs. Similarly, you could bring the inputs and outputs of all your effects, processors and MIDI instruments to a non-normalised patchbay. Other uses for non-normalised patchbays include line level 'tie-lines' – screened cables running from your patchbay to a wallbox in the studio. These may be used for any type of general-purpose connection; for example, you might want to play a guitar in the control room but have it plugged into an amp in the studio. Similarly, you might have synths in the studio area that you want to plug into the mixer in the control room.

logistics

Plan the location of your patchbay to minimise the wiring between it and the rest of your studio equipment. As most patching involves the mixer and the effects rack, it pays to keep them and the patchbay as close together as possible. Use good quality screened cable to wire everything up and keep the leads as short as possible. In the case of insert Y leads (stereo TRS jack at one end, two mono jacks at the other), consider buying ready-made, moulded ones if you don't want to solder up your own.

For the patch leads, choose a soft, non-kinking cable or buy ready-made patch leads, and ensure that they're long enough to reach between the two furthermost sockets on your patchbay system. Coloured leads or plugs help you keep track of what's patched where.

chapter 7

miking techniques

The first 'secret' of miking up an instrument is that the instrument must sound good in the first place. Not only should the instrument be properly maintained, properly tuned and properly played, it should also, where possible, be played in a sympathetic acoustic environment. If something sounds good played in a room, then there's no reason why a good mic placed in the room shouldn't capture that sound quality for you. If the room you have isn't suitable, use a long mic lead and try another room!

With most acoustic instruments, capacitor mics capture the most accurate sound, though you can also get excellent results using back-electret mics or the budget Tandy/Radio Shack PZMs. Dynamic mics can be used to make acceptable recordings, but with quiet instruments, their lack of sensitivity may cause noise problems. Furthermore, because capacitor mics tend to work much better than dynamic mics at the high end of the audio spectrum, bright or detailed sounds are invariably captured more accurately by capacitor mics. Even if you only have access to dynamic mics, still try out the following techniques because you'll still learn a lot, and in most cases the results will be quite good enough for good demo work.

distance

Having got your instrument sounding right in the room, the next question is how far away to put the mic. There are textbook mic positions for most instruments, but it must be stressed that these are just starting points, and the longer you're prepared to experiment, the more successful your recording is likely to be. For example, the acoustic guitar is normally recorded from the front, but I've also miked it successfully from above, over the player's shoulder, working on the theory that if it sounds good to the player, it should also sound good to the mic! All the techniques described here are based on cardioid pattern mics, because that's what most people working at home have access to.

universal mic theory

A real instrument is not a point source of sound – what we hear is a blend of an infinite number of sounds emanating from all parts of the instrument. This means that if the mic is too close to the instrument, you only capture part of the sound; on the other hand, if you put the mic too far away, not only will you be struggling for level, you'll also pick up more reflected room sound than you do direct sound. In some rooms this can sound good, but in most cases, you end up with a boxy, distant sound that's lacking in detail and presence.

A good compromise is to space the mic away from the instrument by a distance similar to the longest dimension of the instrument. In the case of a guitar, you can say that the sound producing part of the instrument is just the body (not strictly true) and put the mic around 400mm from the body, or you could accept that some sound comes directly from the strings and neck and put the mic at up to 800mm from the guitar. If you're working on a drum kit or other collection of percussion instruments and you want to record them with a single mic or stereo pair, then again treat the whole thing as one instrument and space the mic accordingly. In the case of a typical drum kit, the mics would be placed 1-1.5m or so in front of the kit. Though this rule isn't perfect, it will usually get you into the right ball park very quickly, and it's come in very handy when I've been asked to record unusual instruments for which no textbook method exists.

vocals

There's no great mystery to recording vocals, but you do need to pick a location where wall reflections are at a minimum. If necessary, deaden the area by improvising screens with thick blankets or quilts. Set up a cardioid mic so that it points roughly at the singer's nose and use a distance of around 200mm. Even the best vocal mics are prone to popping on B and P sounds, so use a pop shield mid-way between the mic and the singer. Though you can buy pop shields, a piece of stocking material stretched over a wire frame or wooden hoop works just as well. The pop shield diameter should be around 150 to 200mm.

If you have a compressor, try applying gentle compression to the vocals during recording, then add more as you mix. This avoids you overcompressing during recording. Figure 7.1 shows a typical vocal miking position.

drums

Though pro studios tend to mic drum kits using lots of microphones, it's useful to look at the alternative approaches for recording drums, which can vary from one mic per drum to a single mic on the whole kit.

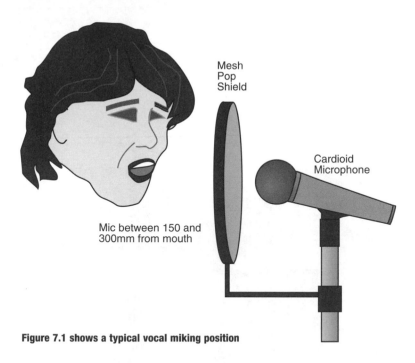

Mesh
Pop
Shield

Cardioid
Microphone

Mic between 150 and
300mm from mouth

Figure 7.1 shows a typical vocal miking position

A good drum sound starts with a good sounding kit, played well. That means having a kit fitted with good heads that have been properly tuned, and a drummer who knows how to hit them to get a happening sound. If the room is too dead, you might also get better results by putting hardboard sheets beneath the kit and around the walls.

If a drum rings too much or if the toms resonate every time you hit the bass drum, pads of folded cloth can be taped to the edges of the heads, but don't kill the sound with too much damping – what might sound like a lot of ring in isolation might be completely hidden in a full mix.

It's possible to get a good drum sound by setting up a pair of mics a few feet in front of the kit, and because this produces a very live sound, this approach has become very fashionable as an alternative to the close-miked drum sound of the eighties and the clinical precision of drum machines. Position the two mics (known in the trade as overheads) between one and two metres from the kit (either in front or above) depending on the acoustic of the room, and space the mics about 1-1.5m apart. As a rule, the more reflective the room, the more exciting the sound will be. Capacitor or back-electret mics are good for this simple approach, and you can also get a good sound from budget PZMs by taping them to the wall behind the kit or by placing them on the floor in front of the kit.

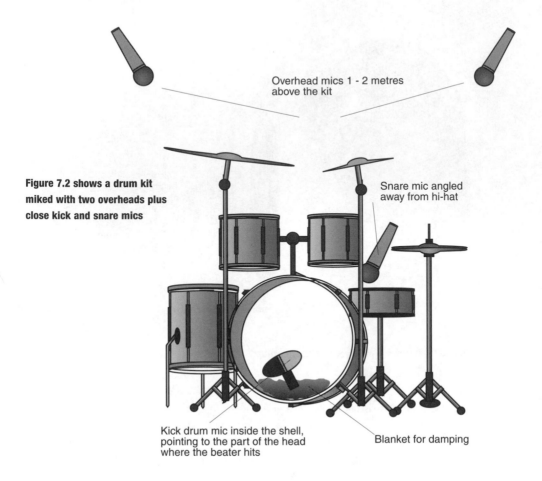

Overhead mics 1 - 2 metres above the kit

Figure 7.2 shows a drum kit miked with two overheads plus close kick and snare mics

Snare mic angled away from hi-hat

Kick drum mic inside the shell, pointing to the part of the head where the beater hits

Blanket for damping

close mics

If the kick drum and snare drum seem to be getting lost, use additional close dynamic mics and bring their level up underneath the stereo mics until you hear a good balance. Mic the bass drum through a hole cut in the front head and place a folded blanket or feather pillow inside the shell to provide some damping. The mic should be about 200mm from the beater, suspended inside the drum shell on a boom stand that isn't physically touching any part of the drum shell. Figure 7.2 shows a drum kit miked with two overheads plus close kick and snare mics.

For the snare, use a dynamic mic around 50mm from the edge of the drum and about 50mm above the head. Try to arrange it so the mic is pointing away from the hi-hat, otherwise you might find the hi-hat overpowers everything. Some engineers like to add a second mic to the snare pointing at the snare head from underneath. I've never had great results doing this, but if you want to give it a try, I suggest you switch the bottom mic out of phase with the top, otherwise the two mics will be trying to cancel each other out.

multiple mics

Most commercial pop recordings are made by miking all the drums separately in which case the toms may be miked in exactly the same way as the snare drum using a single dynamic mic close above the head. If the hi-hats need more prominence, a capacitor or back-electret mic can be set up around 200mm above (or below), and a little to one side, of the hi-hat taking care not to angle directly at the edge of the hi-hats, otherwise you risk picking up the wind noise as the hi-hats close. However you set up the mics, try to make sure they're somewhere where the drummer isn't likely to hit them.

If you're short of tape tracks, at least try to keep the overhead mics on separate tracks, because the way in which these are mixed in with the close mics has a profound effect on the final drum sound. For example, to get a tight, close-miked drum sound, you first get the drums balanced using the close mics, then bring in just a little of the overheads to add air and definition to the cymbals. For a more live sound, on the other hand, start off with the stereo overheads and then use just a little of the close-miked sounds to fine-tune the balance between the various drums.

Close-miked drums usually need some EQ to get the sound just right, and if you have to mix some of the drums as you record, you may have to EQ during recording. If you have the luxury of keeping the drum sounds separate, however, try to save the EQ until you mix.

bass guitar

Most people now record the bass guitar using a DI box or recording preamp, but I've yet to come across one that produces the authority and punch of the real thing. While the bass guitar isn't an acoustic instrument, the bass amplifier/speaker can be considered in exactly the same way as any other instrument.

The best miked bass sounds are usually achieved by putting a good dynamic mic 200 to 300mm from the speaker grille and playing normally. If the cabinet has more than one speaker, listen to them all and if one is better than the others, put the mic close to that speaker. The choice of mic can have a big effect on the sound, and if you want a really deep bass sound, try using a bass drum mic rather than a vocal mic. One tip when recording either electric guitar or bass is to put the amp and mic in a separate room from the one you're monitoring in so that you can hear what the recorded sound is going to be like over the studio monitors.

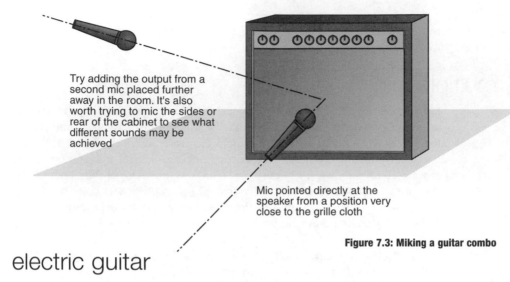

Try adding the output from a second mic placed further away in the room. It's also worth trying to mic the sides or rear of the cabinet to see what different sounds may be achieved

Mic pointed directly at the speaker from a position very close to the grille cloth

Figure 7.3: Miking a guitar combo

electric guitar

At one time, no serious engineer would record the electric guitar any other way than with a mic, but now guitar preamps seem to be just as popular. Even so, there is a real difference in the resulting sound and miking the amp usually produces the best rock or blues sounds.

When you mic an amp, you'll notice the sound changes as you move the mic closer to the speakers and it also gets more mellow as you move away from the centre of the speaker. For rock sounds, put a dynamic mic right up against the grille, and as with the bass guitar, see if any one speaker sounds better than the others. Try to record without additional EQ so that your options are still open when you come to mix. As with recording the bass, try to monitor the to-tape sound in the control room because you'll invariably find that the miked sound is a lot brighter than the perceived sound of the amp. I'd recommend you adjust the tone controls on the amp prior to recording so that the monitored sound is correct rather than simply accepting what you get and then trying to EQ it afterwards.

If you have the facilities, try combining the outputs from two mics, one close and the other further away. It's also worth experimenting by moving the second mic around the sides of the guitar amp, or even placing it behind. If your mixer has a phase switch, listen to see what difference reversing the phase of the distant mic makes.

Figure 7.3 shows how a guitar amp may be miked.

acoustic guitar

Acoustic guitars, especially steel string models, cover a very wide frequency range, so you need to use a fairly sensitive mic with a good high-frequency response if you're to do them justice. You can produce usable results from a good dynamic mic but a capacitor or back-electret model is far preferable. I always used to mic my acoustic guitars in stereo, but the image always seems to lack solidarity. I've now come to the conclusion that if you're going to add stereo reverb anyway, then you might as well record the guitar with a single mic and rely on the reverb to give it space. Again, if you're short on tracks, you'll need to record in mono anyway.

Position the mic around 400mm from the guitar and aim it either at the point where the neck joins the body or at the bridge. Some people aim the mic at the soundhole because that's where most of the sound comes from but, in practice, this usually results in a boomy or boxy sound that needs a lot of EQ to salvage it. The only exception is if you're working with a small scale guitar or one that has a very thin sound, in which case working closer to the soundhole may help fatten the sound up. If you want to try recording in stereo, try a second mic pointing at the centre of the neck from 300 or 400mm away. Because this isn't a 'true' way to record accurate stereo, it doesn't really matter if the two mics are different types, though for all proper stereo applications, it is important that the two mics are identical.

A live acoustic environment is essential for a good acoustic guitar sound, so if your studio is too dead, place a piece of hardboard on the floor or against the wall to reflect some of the sound, just as was suggested in the section on recording drums.

Figure 7.4 shows an acoustic guitar miked with a single microphone.

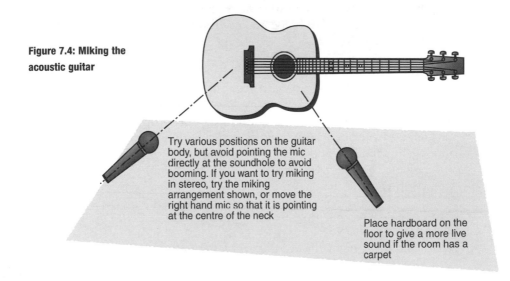

Figure 7.4: Miking the acoustic guitar

Try various positions on the guitar body, but avoid pointing the mic directly at the soundhole to avoid booming. If you want to try miking in stereo, try the miking arrangement shown, or move the right hand mic so that it is pointing at the centre of the neck

Place hardboard on the floor to give a more live sound if the room has a carpet

keyboards

Keyboards, drum machines and samplers may be recorded by plugging them directly into the line inputs of your mixer, but miking an amp can sometimes produce a warmer sound that could be useful to take the edge off digital instruments. In general, keyboard amps are miked a little further back than guitar amps so that the sound from the tweeter is also captured, though for raunchy rock sounds, you can use a guitar amp to add overdrive to the sound and then mic the amp up in exactly the same way as for the guitar.

Miking up keyboards is now the exception rather than the rule, though if you're using a Leslie cabinet, you'll need to use mics to capture the sound. There are many documented ways of miking the Leslie cabinet but the trick seems to be to work in stereo with one mic each side of the cabinet, facing the speaker grilles, and set up not too close, otherwise you pick up wind noise from the rotors and lose the benefit of room reflections. An initial distance of 300 to 400 mm should get you in the right ball park.

wind

Most wind instruments can be successfully recorded by positioning a mic around half a metre in front of the instrument, angled down from above so that the mic isn't pointing directly down the bell or mouth of the instrument. If you're not sure as to the best mic position, go back to the universal mic rule and start from there. I've used this simple rule to make successful recordings of many different instruments including accordions (best use a mic on each side of these) and Irish pipes. I've even recorded the didgeridoo the same way, but in practice, because most of the sound does come out of the end of the pipe and not through the sides, you can afford to get as close as 200mm.

Loud wind instruments, such as the sax, respond well to both capacitor and dynamic mics while flutes seem to sound more open and natural when recorded with a capacitor or back-electret mic. In a pop context, you may find the more punchy, less toppy sound produced by a dynamic mic cuts through a mix better than the more accurate sound of a capacitor mic, so once again, it's a matter of picking what works best on a subjective level.

stereo miking

A successful stereo microphone technique must emulate the way in which we utilise our own two ears to experience sound in a three-dimensional space, and logic might suggest that using two microphones in place of our own ears would be the nearest we could get. This can be tested using a piece of equipment known as a dummy head. If sound is picked up from microphones placed within the ears of a dummy head, then it must be reproduced by loudspeakers in the same physical position as the microphones in order to maintain any degree of accuracy, and the nearest we can get to this in real life is to use headphones. Unfortunately, the technique doesn't work nearly so well when the sound is replayed via loudspeakers.

When we listen to stereo loudspeakers, some of the sound from the left speaker reaches the right ear and vice versa. This introduces a new set of conditions, and different microphone techniques are required. In real life, sound arrives from all directions, but with speakers, all the sound comes from just two locations. Sophisticated though the human hearing system is, it appears to be quite forgiving when it comes to stereophonic sound, and though no man-made recording equals the experience of the live event, even a relatively crude stereo recording can provide a satisfying and pleasurable listening experience.

coincident or xy pair

Possibly the most popular method of stereo miking is the coincident or XY pair. This set-up comprises two identical high-quality cardioid or figure-of-eight mics mounted at approximately 90 degrees to each other and with their capsules as close to each other as is physically possible. As directional microphones are used, one will tend to pick up sound mainly from one side of the soundstage and the other from the opposite side. Figure-of-eight mics will also capture the left and right sound from the rear of the room, including audience noise and room reverberation, though as far as the recording is concerned, these rear sounds will also appear to emanate from the front.

XY provides the necessary change in level from left to right but makes no attempt to account for the masking effect of the human head, or the time delay effects caused by the distance between one ear and the other. However, because cardioids often have a less than perfect high-frequency response when presented with off-axis sounds, the high-frequency attenuation caused by the presence of the human head may, to a degree, be simulated quite by accident!

Because the two microphone capsules are so close to each other that they can be considered coincident (occupying the same space at the same time), all sounds arrive at both capsules at the same time, regardless of their direction; consequently, there are no phase problems that might destroy mono compatibility. However, there are also negative aspects to this arrangement.

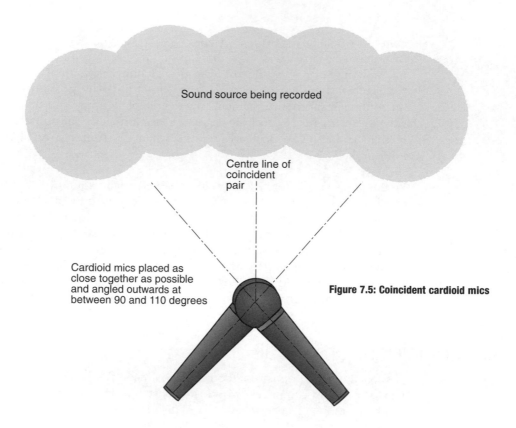

Sound source being recorded

Centre line of
coincident
pair

Cardioid mics placed as
close together as possible
and angled outwards at
between 90 and 110 degrees

Figure 7.5: Coincident cardioid mics

The lack of phase information means that some of the auditory clues we rely on in nature are missing, which results in a 'dilution' of the stereo image. When the two microphones are summed together to provide a mono signal, the lack of phase errors ensures that no significant compatibility problems exist other than those caused by the small physical separation between the capsules. Figure 7.5 shows a coincident pair of cardioid mics.

spaced techniques

So far, we know that coincident miking systems create a level difference between left and right sounds, but no account is taken of the time delay caused by the distance between the ears. We could space the microphones of a coincident pair by a few inches to create an additional sense of space; however, the phase cancellations that occur when the signal is summed to mono cause a degree of coloration, due to the inevitable comb filtering effects brought about by the different times of arrival of off-axis sounds.

A more common approach in professional circles is to use spaced omni microphones, and though the spacing still causes mono compatibility problems, the comb filtering effects seem to be less pronounced. Such a mic arrangement is known as an 'AB Pair' and is extensively used for recordings destined to be replayed over loudspeakers.

The distance of the microphones from the performers must be carefully adjusted, so that the desired balance of direct and reverberant sound is being picked up. If the sound is too ambient, then the mics need to be brought closer to the performers. Conversely, if the sound is too dry, the microphones may be moved further away. Excellent budget recordings may also be made using the inexpensive Tandy PZM microphones in place of conventional omni pattern microphones. Figure 7.6 shows how spaced omni mics might be arranged.

direct-to-stereo recording

If you are working with limited equipment, the simplest way to make a home recording is to use just two microphones to record a complete live performance, directly onto a stereo cassette or open reel recorder. This may sound unsophisticated but it's just about the most accurate way of recording anything. All the best classical recordings are made this way, because by using just a single stereo pair of microphones, we can most

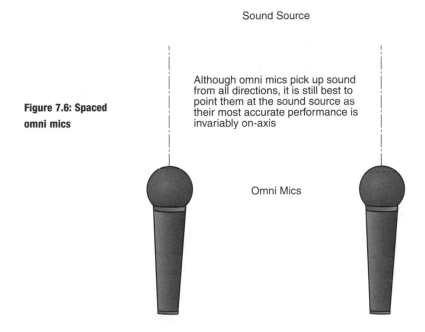

Sound Source

Figure 7.6: Spaced omni mics

Although omni mics pick up sound from all directions, it is still best to point them at the sound source as their most accurate performance is invariably on-axis

Omni Mics

closely approach what a person would actually experience when listening to a live performance.

Of course there are difficulties – the performers have to get the song right all the way through, and the balance between the instruments can't be changed after the recording has been made. Even so, most early records were made that way – many in mono with no EQ! – and they still sound good today.

acoustic music

In the case of acoustic music such as piano or guitar recitals, choirs, chamber music or even folk bands, the direct-to-stereo approach using a single stereo microphone pair can yield excellent results, even when recorded onto a domestic hi-fi cassette recorder. The microphones may be coincident or spaced unidirectional models or even a pair of PZMs fixed to sheets of plywood approximately one metre square.

Given the modest equipment requirements, it is well worth exploring the basic stereo techniques described in this chapter before spending more money on a multitrack system. Good microphones will always be useful, and if you have to buy a decent cassette deck or digital mastering machine especially for the purpose, this can still be used in your multitrack studio for mastering or producing stereo copies.

acoustic environment

The first thing to get right is the actual sound of the musicians, so you need to have them playing in an acoustically sympathetic room with all tuning and maintenance problems taken care of before the session starts. Choirs sound better in reverberant rooms or halls as do string quartets and suchlike, so check your neighbourhood for suitable community halls that don't suffer from excessive outside noise.

Most other instruments also need a live environment to sound their best, but a shorter reverberation time is more normal. For example, to record an acoustic guitar, it may be sufficient to place a sheet of hardboard beneath the player to reflect back some of the sound that would normally be absorbed by the carpet. For home recording, it is worth checking out different rooms to find the one with the best sound, and if you can roll up the carpet in your recording room, then so much the better.

balance

If there are several musicians playing together and there is a problem with one being louder than the others, then your only recourse is to change the position of the musicians relative to the microphones so that the loudest ones are further away. Of course there may be some element of compromise involved because the players will probably want to maintain eye contact with each other to help them with their performance. They'll also need to be spread out from left to right to produce the required stereo picture. As a rule, keep any bass instruments or rhythmic percussion close to the centre.

In the case of a singer/guitarist, the balance between the voice and the guitar can usually be fine-tuned by changing the height of the microphones so they favour either the voice or the instrument as necessary. After each position change, make a short test recording to check the balance and overall sound quality.

mic distance

The amount of reverberation that the room contributes to the recording will be dictated largely by the distance of the microphones from the performers – the closer you get, the more direct sound you'll pick up relative to the room ambience. Conversely, working at a greater distance will give a more reverberant sound but the performance may lose intimacy.

Unless the room has a good live sound, you'll invariably be better off miking fairly close to the instruments to exclude the room sound. If after recording you feel that more ambience would have benefited the performance, you can always copy the tape via a stereo reverb unit to add a little artificial ambience – but take care not to overprocess it.

In finalising the microphone positions when working with ensembles, listen to the musicians run through their performance, close your eyes and concentrate on the sound being produced. Check out different places in the room and see if you can identify 'sweet' spots that seem to sound better than elsewhere, especially if you're recording in a large room or concert hall. Ultimately, if you can find a spot where the performance sounds good to you, it should also sound good to a microphone. If you have access to a good set of enclosed headphones, you can plug these into your recorder to check out the sound that's actually being picked up. This way you'll be able to hear the results of any mic position changes as you make them.

other considerations

Aside from the microphones' distance from the performers, you also have to decide how far to position them from the floor. Ideally the microphones should be higher than the musicians, looking down towards them; this way you'll avoid picking up strong sound reflections from the floor that might adversely colour the sound of your recording.

If you're recording a live concert, you'll also have to find a position that doesn't pick up too much audience noise. Some audience noise will add to the atmosphere of the recording, but the last thing you want is to pick up the conversation of the people sitting closest to the mics. Again you can use height to your advantage and you may even be able to suspend the microphones from the ceiling to avoid your stands obstructing the audience's view.

You'll also need to consider the angle between the microphones, because if it is too large, you may end up with a stereo image that is all left and right with very little in the centre. Conversely, if the angle is too small, the sound will be narrow, almost like mono. As a rule, the mics should point roughly between the centre of the stage and the performers at the outside of the group. This same general rule applies if you decide to use spaced microphones rather than a coincident pair. Even so, every recording is different so don't be afraid to use your ears and move the mics about until you're happy with the result. Figure 7.7 illustrates a typical spaced mic arrangement for recording an ensemble.

multi-mic methods

Pop and rock music is less easy to record with just two microphones because the balance between the instruments is not a natural one – after all, the unamplified human voice could never compete with a drum kit. Likewise, many of the instruments, such as electric guitars and basses or electronic keyboards, are only designed to be used with amplification. Certainly it is possible to balance the levels of all the different instrument amplifiers and then record the result, but the main problem is that amplified vocals are rarely of sufficient quality to record. Nevertheless, if you have a decent sounding PA system, by all means give it a try – the experience will always be worthwhile and the results may be quite adequate to use as demos.

A better solution is to use a small mixer and several different microphones, so that the various elements of the performance can be balanced prior to recording. You'll need to use a number of mics on the drums – a minimum of two overheads, but ideally close mics on the snare and kick drum too. Some of the sound from the other instruments will inevitably get into the drum mics, but this needn't be too serious. In the event that the players are packed close together because of space constraints, it is advantageous to improvise acoustic screens to separate the drums and amplifiers from each other by draping heavy blankets or sleeping bags over clothes drying frames, mic stands or other impromptu structures. This won't cure sound spillage completely but may make the difference between a situation that is viable and one that isn't.

vintage recordings

Harking back to the old days of direct-to-stereo pop recording, this was achieved using a simple mixing console similar to the ones used for small live performances today. Separate microphones would be used for the main instruments or groups of instruments, and then their levels would be balanced at the mixer. The singer would also sing into a microphone plugged into the mixer and a headphone mix would be provided for monitoring.

These early mixers had no EQ so if the engineer wanted to change the tone of something, he'd have to move the mic around or even try a different type of microphone. Reverb was usually created using specially built live rooms, and to multitrack an instrument, several players would be hired in to play the same part at the same time. Obviously, the fact that the mixers available to us have all got some form of equalisation and the availability of inexpensive effects units puts us at quite an advantage over these pioneers.

If you want to try multi-mic recording for yourself with the minimum of equipment, I'd recommend close-miking the instruments in the band but have the singer in a totally separate room monitoring the sound going to tape via headphones, preferably the fully enclosed type of phones that don't allow much sound to leak out. This method means that bands have to learn the song well enough to play it without hearing the vocals or even seeing the vocalist, but that should be no problem for competent players. The engineer, the mixer and the stereo recorder are then located in a third room so that the engineer can hear the performance as it sounds over monitor speakers or headphones without interference from the performance itself.

Because modern mixers allow us the luxury of stereo panning, it is possible to create some kind of stereo picture, but do keep all the bass sounds such as bass guitar and bass drum near the centre of the mix.

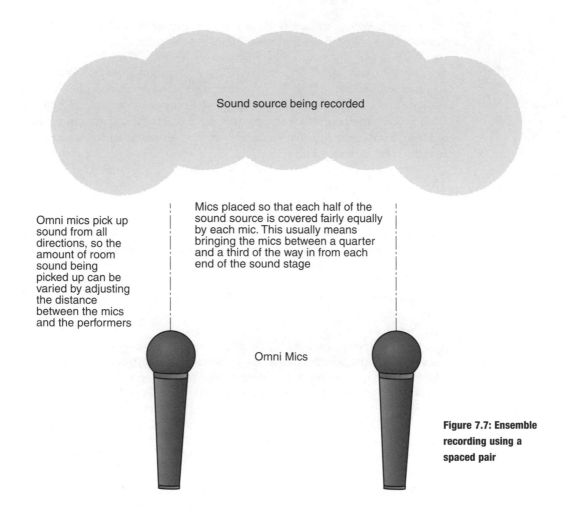

Sound source being recorded

Omni mics pick up sound from all directions, so the amount of room sound being picked up can be varied by adjusting the distance between the mics and the performers

Mics placed so that each half of the sound source is covered fairly equally by each mic. This usually means bringing the mics between a quarter and a third of the way in from each end of the sound stage

Omni Mics

Figure 7.7: Ensemble recording using a spaced pair

Failure to do this will result in a less powerful sound and the uneven left/right balance rarely sounds artistically pleasing. For a full description on setting up a musically pleasing balance, refer to the chapter on mixing.

adding effects

If any effects are required, these must be added at the mixer before the recording takes place, though you can probably get away with just a little reverb on the vocals. The effects would be patched into the effects send/return circuit just as they would for a live performance. If you have more sophisticated signal processing at your disposal such as a reasonable compressor, then it would be a good idea to use this to keep the vocal level even by patching it into the insert point of the channel handling the lead vocal mic. Compressors are discussed in more detail in the section on Effects and Processors.

Because the recording can't be changed at all once it is complete, the players must be made aware that mistakes or balance problems can't be corrected afterwards and they should also be cautioned to stay quiet after the recording has finished. Solos should also be worked out, at least for length, because there will be no way for the guitar player to give a knowing nod to the singer when he feels he's expressed himself enough.

sequencers

Though this is essentially a chapter on microphones and their applications, an interesting variation on the 'direct to stereo' theme involves the use of MIDI sequencer. If you're one of those musicians who feels quite at home creating entire backing tracks using sequenced drum machines, synths and samplers, then these can take the place of your live band when you come to do your recording. In other words, you'll be recording live instruments and vocals via mics at the same time as recording the backing from your sequencer. You'll still need to get the vocals right first time, as you will any instruments you intend to add live, but at least you know your 'band' will deliver perfect performances indefinitely and without complaint until you're happy with the result. I like to think of this method of recording as the modern equivalent of a vintage 'direct to stereo' session where session musicians were used to play the backing.

If you can overcome the attitude that all good recordings must be made using multitrack, you can achieve first rate results by going direct to stereo, especially if you have access to an open-reel or DAT stereo recorder. It does demand a more disciplined musical approach but you cut out a whole generation of recording and the quality loss that entails. It also does wonders for your musical ability – multitrack recording and computer sequencing have become a crutch for a great many musicians and their performing ability has suffered because of it.

summary

If you play a musical instrument, you probably practise on a regular basis, and the same should be true of your recording techniques. Don't wait until you have a record to make to try out new mic techniques – set aside an hour or two and just experiment with a few things to see what different results you can come up with. In particular, try to assess the effect of changing the mic type and distance. One way of doing this is to monitor the results via enclosed headphones as you physically move the mic. With just a little persistence, you can maintain the more traditional recording skills as well as making the most of what modern synth and sampler technology has to offer.

chapter 8

effects and processors

why do we need them?

One of the problems of recording in a home studio is that everything sounds small because your recording space doesn't have the same acoustic ambience as a concert hall or club. In fact the same is true of most professional studios apart from those with large, live rooms, and most pop music is recorded fairly 'dry', either in a fairly dead environment or by close miking. Electronic effects units are then used to recreate the desired ambience, and the most important effects unit of them all is reverberation or reverb.

Reverberation occurs naturally when sound is reflected and re-reflected from walls and other obstacles within a large room, and an electronic reverb unit mimics this effect by generating thousands of reflections electronically. Like all modern day effects, reverb can be used to create the impression of a real room, but it may also be used to create new effects that have no obvious counterpart in nature.

Effects are very powerful tools, but if you try to use them to cover up a poor recording, you won't fool anyone. A good mix always starts with a good recording of a good performance.

If you do all your recording dry, adding effects only when you mix, you have the advantage that you can experiment with different types of effect after the recording has been made. In the professional studio where there's a big mixer, lots of tape tracks and plenty of different effects units, that's quite feasible, but in a small home studio, it's often more practical to add some of the effect as you record and others as you mix.

If you're working with a 4-track system for example, you often have to bounce tracks, which means that if you want the individual sounds to have different effects, you'll have to add these as you bounce. You may also find that your multitrack workstation doesn't have as many effects sends and returns as you need, so it's quite possible that some of the effects will have to be added when you first record the parts.

Guitar effects are usually recorded to tape because they affect the way the guitarist plays. Even so, it helps if you can leave putting the reverb on until last. Not only does this let you find the right effects type and effects balance, but it also enables you to keep the reverb in stereo which does much to create the feeling of space and depth within a mix. Usually, effects added at the recording stage will be in mono because you simply can't afford the tape tracks to keep everything in stereo, but if you add a little stereo reverb at the final mixing stage, you'll be surprised at how the sound takes on new depth and realism.

main studio effects
reverberation

Reverberation is closely linked with the way in which we perceive sound and it contains clues which our subconscious uses to determine such things as direction, type of acoustic environment and distance.

As touched upon earlier, reverberation occurs naturally when a sound bounces from the surfaces within a room, and its effect is evident as a series of closely spaced echoes following the original sound. If you were to examine the individual reflections that make up natural reverb, you'd discover that after the initial sound, there's a short pause as the sound travels to the nearest surfaces (walls, floors and ceilings), then bounces back to the listener. After that, closely spaced reflections or echoes bounce back, but some of these encounter other surfaces and are re-reflected.

As time elapses, the complexity of the reflections builds up rapidly so that the individual echoes are no longer audible, and because natural materials absorb sound as well as reflect it, the intensity of the reflections dies away. With most materials, the high frequencies are absorbed more readily than low frequencies, so as the reverb decays, so it becomes duller sounding. Different types of rooms and different materials produce different sounds, which is why modern reverberation units provide a number of room types and user-adjustable parameters.

The time taken for a reverb to fall in level by 60dB (which effectively means to near silence), is known as the decay time, and most musical applications require a fairly short reverb time of between one and three seconds, though digital reverbs can also emulate huge caverns with decay times of ten seconds or even more. Plate settings are popular for general use, especially on vocals and drums, the term plate referring to the mechanical reverb plate that was used before digital reverb units were invented .

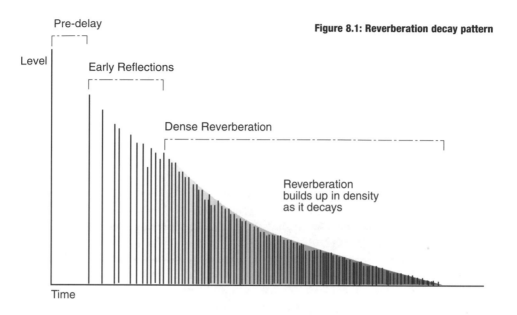

Figure 8.1: Reverberation decay pattern

In real life, you hear a different pattern of reverb reflections with each ear and that's what provides the brain with stereo information. Even if the sound source is mono, for example a single voice or hand clap, the reverberation will always be stereo. Digital reverb units process a mono input to produce two different sets of synthetic reflections in order to produce a convincing stereo effect. Figure 8.1 shows the pattern of decaying reflections created by a typical digital reverberation unit.

reverb patching

Effects such as reverb are normally fed from a post-fade send control (effects send), which means that the reverb level will increase and decrease along with the original sound if the channel fader is moved. This is obviously the way you'd normally want to work, though you can drive a reverb unit from a pre-fade send if you want to fade out the dry signal while still leaving the reverb audible – something you may want to do to create an unusual or special effect.

The advantage of the aux send system is that it allows the same effects device to be shared among all the mixer channels while still allowing you to have different amounts of effect on each channel. For example, you might be able to use the same reverb setting on both drums and vocals, but you may want to use more on the vocals than on the drums.

To maintain a stereo effect while mixing, the reverb left and right outputs should be panned hard left and right, in the mix. A multitrack workstation with stereo effects returns will automatically pan the effects return signals left and right, but if you're using spare input channels, you'll have to remember to do this manually. The effects unit output mix parameter or control is then set for effect only – no dry signal. If you use input channels as returns, ensure that the corresponding aux send is turned completely off on those channels, otherwise some of the reverb gets fed back to its own input causing feedback of tonal coloration.

To make sure your reverb unit (or multi-effects processor) works as quietly as possible (remember gain structure?), set the aux sends on the channels you want to effect to around three quarters full up. The aux send master should also be set to three quarters full up – the input level control on the effects unit itself is used to set the signal level going into the unit so that a healthy meter reading is obtained. You should set the output level of the effects unit to be close to maximum and then adjust the effects return level on the mixer to give you the right subjective level of effect.

To keep unwanted noise to an absolute minimum, it's important to turn down any post-fade aux sends that aren't being used and to de-route any mixer channels that aren't being used in the mix. This doesn't just mean turning the fader down – you should also mute the channel. If you are using a console with routing buttons, also make sure that unused channels aren't routed to the main stereo mix. It's not often realised that a muted channel with the fader down will still contribute a little noise (known as mix buss noise) just from being connected to the stereo mix buss.

If you're using a separate studio mixer and you want to add a specific effect to only one channel, you can take your effects send from the channel's insert send or from the channel's direct output if it has one. This removes the contribution of mix buss noise altogether. Alternatively, feed the signal to be treated directly from your multitrack recorder into the effects unit, then feed the effects unit outputs into two adjacent mixer channels panned hard left and right. The effect/mix balance will then have to be set on the effects unit.

If all the effects sends are in use, effects may be connected via insert points, though this limits their use to that one channel only. When working in the aux send/return mode, the dry sound should be turned off on the effects unit. When used via an insert point, the effect/dry balance must be set on the effects unit itself.

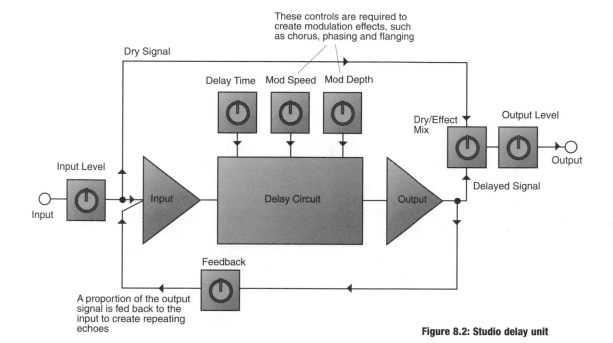

Figure 8.2: Studio delay unit

delay

Delay, as the name suggests, is a means of delaying an audio signal so as to produce one or more distinct echoes. By feeding some of the delayed sound back to the input, the echoes continue to recirculate and decay, creating multiple echoes. The higher the level of the feedback, the longer the echoes take to decay. The main parameters are delay time and feedback. Figure 8.2 shows a block diagram of a delay unit.

multi-tapped delay

Modern multi-effects units often include multi-tapped delay programs that generate multiple echoes at different delay times. It may also be possible to pan the individual delays from left to right in the stereo field to create interesting, spacial effects.

A popular technique is to set the echo delay time so that the repeats are in time with the tempo of the song, though shorter delays can be used to create a doubling or double-tracking effect. Echo effects were popular back in the sixties and early seventies where they were often used on lead guitar and vocals. Today the effect is still popular, and is used on all types of instrument and voice.

modulation effects

It's surprising how many of the standard studio effects are variations on the digital delay theme, where the delay time is modulated by a low frequency oscillator to produce chorus, flanging, phasing and vibrato effects. Modulation, in this context, simply means that the delay time is varied under the control of a low frequency oscillator. Some modulation effects, such as phasing, use such short delay times that no delay is perceptible, while chorus and ADT use a slightly longer delay time to produce a doubling or thickening effect.

chorus and adt

Chorus uses a short delay up to about 70mS to create a slight doubling effect, and the delay time is then modulated to produce a slight wavering in pitch. An equal mix of the delayed and unprocessed sound is used to produce an effect rather like two instruments playing the same part but with slight differences in timing and tuning. This characteristic makes chorus useful for creating ensemble effects from single instruments.

The chorus depth is controlled by the LFO (Low Frequency Oscillator), modulation depth and, as a rule, the faster the modulation, the less depth is needed. Chorus is often used on string sounds, synthesizer pads, electric guitars and fretless bass guitars.

ADT or Automatic Double Tracking is similar to chorus but uses a delay time in excess of 70mS to create more pronounced doubling or 'slapback' effect, and the depth of modulation is less. ADT is often used to process vocals to make it appear that the same singer has performed the part twice, on different tape tracks, again to obtain a thicker sound. The amount of modulation should be so slight as to be only just noticeable.

flanging

Flanging is closely related to chorusing but uses shorter delay times with the addition of feedback to create an effect similar to classic tape flanging. The higher the feedback setting, the stronger the effect, and as with chorus, faster speed should be used with reduced depth. Both chorus and flanging sound best in stereo if your effects unit has that capability.

Flanging sounds good on vocals, bass, synthesizer and even drums, but because it is such a dramatic effect, it is best used sparingly. The more harmonically rich the original sound, the more pronounced the flanging effect.

phasing

Phasing uses shorter delay times than flanging and little or no feedback to produce a moving comb filter which sounds not unlike mild flanging. Because the effect is more subtle than flanging, it can be used more extensively and many Pink Floyd tracks feature phasing on the lead guitar.

vibrato

Vibrato is a modulation of pitch similar to that produced manually by a guitar or violin player and is created by using only the delayed sound and none of the original. The delay is kept to just a few mS so as not to significantly affect the timing of the performance, and the modulation depth sets the vibrato depth.

pitch shifting

Pitch shifters can change the pitch of the original signal but without changing the speed of the sound, and they usually have a maximum range of at least one octave up and down. Pitch shifting is often found in the modulation section of multi-effects units, but it isn't a modulated delay process at all. Pitch shifting works by breaking the sound into very short segments and sampling them in turn. Each sample is then either looped or truncated depending on whether the pitch is being moved up or down and digital algorithms are used to splice the segments back together so as to avoid glitching. Most low cost pitch shifters impart a strange timbre caused by the regular modulation of the looping and splicing processes, but if mixed with the original sound, this side effect can be disguised. There's also a slight delay due to the sampling and splicing process, but this can be as short as just a few milliseconds.

Smaller pitch shifts sound very similar to chorus effects, but without the regular modulation of chorus. Such 'detuning' treatments, combined with a short delay, are often used to double or thicken vocals. Larger shifts can be used to create octaves or parallel harmonies, and so-called intelligent pitch shifters can be set to add musically correct, real-time harmonies to vocal or guitar parts. Interesting effects may also be achieved by pitch shifting percussive sounds to create deep snare and kick drum sounds.

The newest pitch shifting feature is 'format correction', whereby the character of a voice can be altered without changing the speed or, alternatively, the pitch of a voice can be changed without the usual Mickey

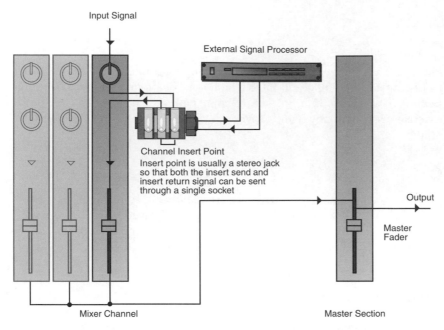

Connection via insert point

Figure 8.3: Processor and Effect signal paths

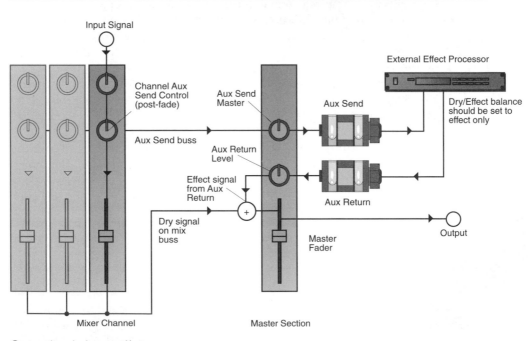

Connection via Aux send/return

Mouse effect. It is anticipated that future developments in this area will allow singers to change their voices so as to sound more like the artistes they are covering.

aux sends and inserts

Delay or reverb-type effects can be connected either to an aux send or an insert point, but there are other processing devices which don't have the same flexibility when it comes to patching. Reverb and delay effects are usually added to the original signal so that you hear both together, but when you put a signal though an equaliser, the whole signal is affected – no untreated sound is heard at all. To avoid confusion, it helps if you mentally divide your outboard devices into two categories: 'effects' should be reserved to describe those devices that rely on some form of delay circuitry to make them operate while the other category, 'processors', describes the type of device that processes the entire signal, changing it either tonally or in level. Another clue when deciding which device belongs in which category is that effects usually have some form of dry/effects balance control whereas processors (with the possible exception of exciters) do not. Processors should only be connected via insert points or between the line output of one piece of equipment and the line input of another whereas Effects can be connected both via insert points and aux sends.

Effects based on delay circuitry include reverb, delay, echo, chorus, flanging, vibrato and pitch shift. When used in the aux send system of a mixing console, the dry signal level should be turned right down at the effects unit and the effect level set to maximum. The amount of effect added to each mixer channel is then determined by the channel aux send control.

If insert points are used to connect effects, the dry/effects balance must be set at the effects unit.

processors

Those devices categorised as processors include exciters, equalisers, compressors, limiters, gates, expanders and auto-panners. These change either the level or the tonal quality of the signal passing through them and you wouldn't normally add a dry signal to the output of one of these units. Because aux sends are used to add the output from an effect to the dry signal, it isn't normal to connect a processor via an aux send.

Figure 8.3 shows the difference in the signal paths of a processor and an effect.

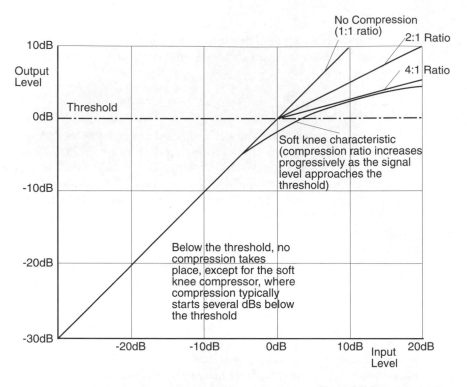

No Compression
(1:1 ratio)

2:1 Ratio

4:1 Ratio

10dB

Output
Level

Threshold

0dB

Soft knee characteristic
(compression ratio increases
progressively as the signal
level approaches the
threshold)

-10dB

Below the threshold, no
compression takes
place, except for the soft
knee compressor, where
compression typically
starts several dBs below
the threshold

-20dB

-30dB

-20dB   -10dB   0dB   10dB   Input   20dB
                                  Level

Figure 8.4: Compressor ratio graph

compressor/limiter

Compressors are used to 'even out' excessive peaks in signal level that occur in vocal or instrumental performances, and they do this by changing the gain of the signal path depending on the level of the signal passing through. Just as an engineer might pull down a fader if the level gets too high, so a compressor will turn down the level if it exceeds a threshold set by the user. Signals falling below the threshold level remain unchanged. The degree of gain reduction applied is set by the compression Ratio control setting as shown in the graph in Figure 8.4.

When the ratio is very high, the compressor's maximum output is maintained at the threshold level and is effectively prevented from going beyond it. This sets a limit on the maximum signal level regardless of the input, and a compressor used with a high ratio setting is often described as a limiter, hence the term Compressor/Limiter. As a rule, high compression ratios are used in conjunction with high threshold settings so that only the signal peaks are affected. Lower ratios may be used with lower threshold settings to provide gain levelling over a greater dynamic range.

The compressor's Attack control determines how quickly the circuitry responds once a signal has exceeded the threshold while Release sets the time for the gain to return to normal once the input has dropped back below the threshold. Some compressors have auto attack and release settings that respond to the dynamic character of the input signal. Auto mode is very useful for processing signals with constantly changing characteristics, such as vocals, slap/pull bass guitar or complete mixes.

Most 2-channel compressors have a Stereo Link switch so that stereo signals can be processed. In link mode, both channels are compressed by the same amount which prevents the image appearing to move to one side or the other when a loud sound appears only on one side of the mix.

The maximum gain of a compressor occurs when the input signal is below the threshold which can sometimes lead to background noise being boosted during quiet passages or pauses. To combat this problem, some compressors are provided with built-in gates so that the signal may be silenced during pauses.

Compressors are most often used to keep instrument and vocal levels at an even volume during a mix though they may also be used to add sustain to guitars. Setting a deliberately long attack time can also help emphasise the attack of a sound such as the slap of bass guitar.

Limiting is used in circumstances where it would be undesirable for a signal to exceed a specific level – for example, to prevent clipping on a digital recorder.

gates

Whereas compressors control the level of signals that exceed a threshold, gates control the level of signals that fall below a threshold. The aim is to silence the signal during pauses when any background noise will not be masked by the presence of a signal. If the gate threshold level is set just above the background noise, the gate will operate whenever there is a pause in the signal.

Gates are used for muting the spill from other instruments as well as for tackling straightforward noise or hiss problems and they are regularly used when miking drum kits to prevent, for example, the bass drum mic from picking up the other drums in the kit. They are also often used with electric guitars to combat the high level of noise and hum generated by a typical guitar amplifier when the guitarist is not actually playing. Vocals may be gated to hide any rustling clothing sounds or unwanted breathing.

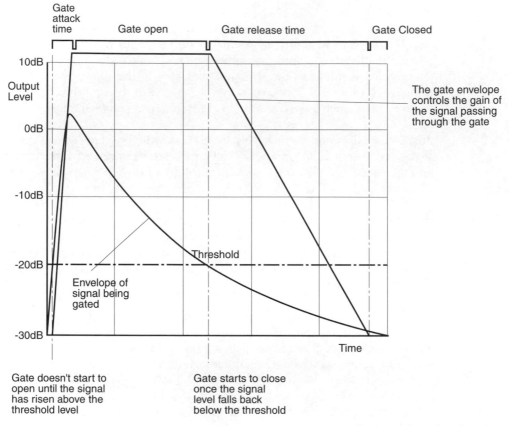

Figure 8.5: Operation of a gate

It must be understood that gates only remove noise when there is a pause in the wanted signal – they can't help with noise that's audible over the top of the programme material. Even so, using gates on all the noisy tracks in a multitrack recording can help produce a much cleaner sounding recording. Figure 8.5 shows how a gate reacts when the signal falls below the threshold level. Expanders are very similar to gates except that they close down gently, more like a compressor in reverse.

equalisers

Equalisers are essentially tone controls, and the different types are described in the chapter on equalisation. Most mixers have EQ built in, but it's often useful to have a better quality external equaliser that can be patched in via an insert point for those occasions where more precise control is required. Parametric equalisers are the most versatile, but also the most time consuming to set up properly.

exciters

Also known as enhancers, exciters are devices that add synthesized high frequency harmonics to a signal to make it sound brighter and more intimate than it originally did. The process was developed and patented by Aphex, and is different to equalisation, which only redistributes the harmonics that already exist. Exciters are used to push sounds to the front of the mix or to create clarity and space in crowded mixes. They can be used on whole mixes or just on individual tracks and may also be used to brighten stereo mixes destined as masters for cassette copying in order to help compensate for the loss of high frequency content that cassette duplication often entails. Enhancers working on slightly different principles are available from other manufacturers.

autopanners

An autopanner is simply a device that automatically pans a mono signal from left to right in the mix, usually under the control of a low frequency oscillator or external trigger. Used in time with the tempo of a track, panning can be quite subtle. Many multi-effects units include a panning facility as well as a rotary speaker emulator, a setting designed to simulate Leslie speakers and similar systems that employ rotating baffles to add vibrato to organ sounds. Most rotary speaker sounds combine panning with chorus, and they often have two speeds with a delayed speed up and slow down function to mimic the mechanical inertia of the real thing.

patching

Patching effects can be confusing to newcomers, so I've included this list of key points for reference.

★ Insert points are invariably presented as stereo jacks wired to carry both the send and return signal, so if you don't have a patchbay, you'll need a Y lead with a stereo jack on one end and two monos on the other.

★ Processors must always be used 'in-line' with a signal and not in the effects send/return loop unless you really know exactly what you are doing and why you're doing it.

★ Most processors work at line level, so you can't plug a mic directly into them. The correct way to, for example, compress a mic signal, is to patch the compressor into the insert point of the mic channel. This way, the mixer's mic amp brings the mic signal up to line level before feeding it to the compressor.

★ If an effect is used via the aux/send return system, it is normal to set the FX unit's dry/effect balance to 'effect only' so as to allow the console's aux send controls to control the effect balance.

★ Some effects, such as phasing and flanging, rely on a precise effect/dry balance which may be better accomplished in the effects unit itself. In this case, either patch the FX unit into an insert point or, if you must use the aux/send system, you can either de-route the channel from the stereo mix to kill the dry signal, or feed the effects unit from a pre-fade (foldback) send and turn the channel fader right down.

★ To use a mono-in, stereo-out FX unit (such as reverb or stereo delay) via insert points, simply route one output of the unit to the insert return of the channel feeding it and the other to the insert return of an adjacent channel. Match the levels, pan one track hard left and the other hard right for maximum stereo effect.

★ To use a stereo-in, stereo-out FX unit via insert points, use two adjacent mixer channels panned hard left and right.

★ To treat a whole mix, say with EQ or compression, patch your processor into the master insert points. This places your unit in the signal path just before the master stereo faders which means that if you're using a compressor, it won't try to fight you if you do a fadeout. Similarly, any noise generated by the processor will also be faded as you pull the faders down.

★ If you don't have Master insert points, you can patch a processor between the mixer's stereo out and the input to your stereo mastering recorder, but if you want to do fades with a compressor patched in, you'll need to do them using the input level control on the tape machine, not on the desk.

summary

Effects are essential to modern recording, with reverberation being the most important effect of all. Fortunately, good multi-effects units are now relatively cheap, but if one unit is all you can afford, make sure it can deliver smooth, natural reverb as well as the more dramatic multi-effects. Poor quality reverb units tend to have a metallic ring to them when percussive sounds, such as snare drums, are being treated.

chapter 9

introducing midi

MIDI is an integral part of contemporary music making, but I remember that when I first encountered it, I thought that it was very much more complicated than actually turned out to be the case. Of course there's no need to use MIDI at all if you're only recording conventional instruments, but in practice, the majority of commercial recordings usc both MIDI and 'real' sound sources. MIDI will be covered more thoroughly in another book in this series, but the following chapter should provide you with enough background information to get started.

Part of the problem with MIDI is the jargon that goes with it, but some people harbour a suspicion that MIDI and computers mean handing over the musical process to a machine. On top of that, it's not always made clear exactly what MIDI can do for the musician. To tackle the first question first, is MIDI really complicated?

MIDI is complicated in the same way that a car engine or a telephone exchange is complicated, but you don't have to be a car mechanic to drive a car, or an electronics engineer to use a telephone. MIDI is just another creative tool and you can either use it simply or to perform complex tasks – you are in control.

what midi does

MIDI is often defined as a communication protocol for use with musical instruments, but that definition is of little help to the newcomer. What this really means is that MIDI is a common electronic protocol that enables two or more MIDI-equipped electronic instruments to be linked together in such a way that musical information can pass from one to the other. I'll come onto the definition of musical information shortly. MIDI stands for Musical Instrument Digital Interface, but you don't have to know anything about digital electronics to use it. In fact, from the user's point of view, MIDI has more in common with telephones and TV remote controls.

MIDI instruments, and other MIDI devices, are equipped with 5-pin DIN sockets to handle the MIDI data, and on a typical unit, you will see sockets marked MIDI In, MIDI Out and MIDI Thru. These sockets are connected using standard MIDI cables but there are a few simple rules as to what should be plugged where. I shall cover these a little later.

First of all, I'd like to elaborate on this mysterious information that is passed from one device to another via MIDI. There are many types of MIDI message so I'll start by covering the most obvious ones first. MIDI instruments are electronic, which means that the sound you hear is created electronically, not by a mechanical action as in the case of a piano or guitar. In other words, the keys on an electronic instrument are little more than switches that generate electronic signals to tell the instrument's circuitry what note to play and how loud to play it. Whenever a key is pressed on a MIDI synthesizer, a signal known as a Note On message is sent, and when the key is released, a second message is sent known as a Note Off. The pitch of the note being played is generally related to which key you hit, just as it is on a piano, and the faster or harder you hit the key, the louder the sound is. Because playing 'hardness' is really the same thing as speed as far as the key is concerned, we call the 'hardness' of playing 'velocity'. This is an often used piece of MIDI jargon so it's worth remembering.

Quick Recap: So far, we know that a musical note transmitted over MIDI comprises a Note On message, the pitch of the note, the loudness of the note and a Note Off message. There are other things that you can do to a note, such as bending the pitch or adding vibrato, but the main thing to grasp at the moment is that every time you press down a key on a MIDI keyboard, information is generated defining the note, its duration and its loudness.

The next conceptual leap is to take this electronic pitch, Note On, Note Off and velocity information and send it down a MIDI cable so that it can control a remote MIDI instrument that may be at the other side of the room. This may not seem particularly useful just yet, but this concept is the basis of MIDI and its applications.

MIDI isn't a means of transmitting sounds directly – it's a system for transmitting instructions about what is happening on the master keyboard. One analogy is the written musical score; this only tells the performer what notes to play and when to play them, it can't affect the sound of the instrument or even what instrument you decide to play that music on.

midi connections

To make a basic MIDI connection, plug the MIDI Out of the keyboard (the instrument you are actually playing), to the MIDI In socket of a second MIDI

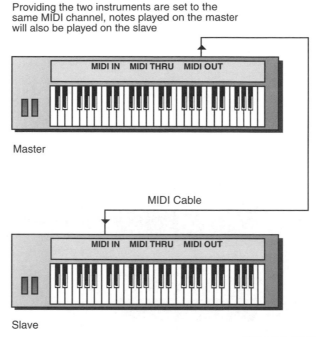

Providing the two instruments are set to the same MIDI channel, notes played on the master will also be played on the slave

Master

MIDI Cable

Slave

Figure 9.1: Basic MIDI connection

instrument, known as the slave. This is shown in Figure 9.1. Now, when you play a note on the master keyboard, the slave instrument will also play, providing both instruments arc set to the same MIDI channel.

midi channels

To connect more MIDI instruments together, the MIDI Thru of the first slave is connected to the MIDI In of the second slave and so on, and in such a system, all the modules receive the same MIDI information at the same time. However, most of the time, we want the MIDI data to be played back by only one of several modules in the system, which is why MIDI channels are needed.

There are 16 MIDI channels and they work in a very similar way to TV channels insomuch as all TV channels are picked up by the same aerial, yet we can still switch channels to watch just the one we want. With MIDI, information can bc sent on any one of 16 channels (something you can select on the master keyboard), and the sound modules making up the rest of the system may each be set to receive on any one of the 16 channels. (Most modules have a MIDI mode called Omni which allows them to respond to all 16 MIDI channels at once, but this is of little use in normal situations.)

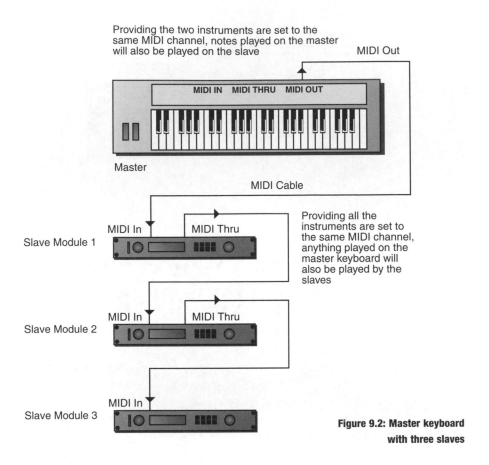

Providing the two instruments are set to the
same MIDI channel, notes played on the master
will also be played on the slave

MIDI Out

MIDI IN   MIDI THRU   MIDI OUT

Master

MIDI Cable

Slave Module 1
MIDI In   MIDI Thru

Providing all the
instruments are set to
the same MIDI channel,
anything played on the
master keyboard will
also be played by the
slaves

Slave Module 2
MIDI In   MIDI Thru

Slave Module 3
MIDI In

**Figure 9.2: Master keyboard
with three slaves**

If the master keyboard is set to transmit on MIDI channel 1 and connected
to two different MIDI modules set to receive on channels 1 and 2, only the
module set to channel 1 will respond (providing module 2 hasn't been
accidentally set to Omni mode). Both modules still receive the information,
but unless the MIDI transmit and receive channels are the same, it will be
ignored. You could put two or more modules on the same MIDI channel for
layering sounds, but in most systems, each sound module would be set to a
different MIDI channel.

By selecting different channels on the master keyboard, up to 16 different
modules, each set to its own MIDI channel, can be controlled individually.
Figure 9.2 shows a master keyboard connected to three slaves.

sound modules

A MIDI sound module is really just a MIDI instrument without a keyboard, but most modern instruments and modules can play several different sounds at once, each on its own MIDI channel. In other words, you might find the box you have bought isn't just one musical instrument but as many as 16 different MIDI instruments all sharing the same box. A MIDI module or keyboard that can behave as several different instruments at the same time is said to be multitimbral. However, the different instruments inside the box are not usually totally independent; they invariably share the same set of front panel controls and the sound outputs may be internally mixed so that everything comes out via a single stereo pair of output sockets.

On more expensive instruments there may be more outputs to which the individual musical parts can be directed, but few instruments have more than eight separate outputs. You can change the relative levels and pan positions of the various parts using the front panel controls, so having everything mixed to one stereo output isn't as big a restriction as it might at first appear.

sequencers

If up until now you've been a live performer, you might wonder why you need 16 different instruments in one box because surely you can only play one at a time given the limitation of a single pair of hands? Well, you could split your keyboard and have something like a bass instrument on the bottom two octaves and maybe a piano on the rest, but even that doesn't need 16-part multitimbrality.

The answer of course is the MIDI sequencer which can play all 16 parts together with no effort. Using a sequencer, just one multitimbral module can provide you with a complete backing track, including the drums. Before MIDI, few people could compose a symphony, or pop song for that matter, and ever expect to hear it performed, but now almost anyone can turn their musical ideas into a performance using affordable technology.

The traditional way to create music is to compose a score, then once the score is finished, you hire an orchestra and get them to play what you've written. As with the orchestral composer, sequencer-based work usually starts at the keyboard, but this time the keyboard is a MIDI instrument connected to a MIDI sequencer. Instead of writing down a score, the composer will record sections of the music into the sequencer against an electronic metronome set to the desired tempo, and instead of scanning a score to verify what's been done, it's a simple matter to play back the recording to hear exactly what has been recorded. Best of all, you don't have to hire in an orchestra because a relatively inexpensive multitimbral synthesizer will provide all the sounds for you; each 'part' of the multitimbral synth plays one line of your electronic score. If the end result isn't quite right, you can make changes without having to hire the orchestra again to confirm that your changes are okay. To make changes, you simply erase or move the unwanted notes and add new ones.

It's often convenient to visualise a sequencer as being something like a multitrack tape recorder, which is fine so long as you don't go back to thinking about recording sounds – MIDI is all about data or instructions that tell your instruments what to play. Just as a musical score is a series of instructions to the musicians, a MIDI sequence holds a series of instructions which tell your synths what to play.

In some ways, the sequencer is better than the written score because it can play back a part exactly as you played it in the first place – it doesn't have to 'quantise' everything to equal subdivisions of a musical bar as the written score does.

In reality, MIDI does have a finite timing resolution because the computer has to work to an internal timing routine based on an electronic clock, but in practice, MIDI is far more accurate than a typical human performer and is capable of resolving a bar of music into at least 960 time divisions and frequently more.

Some software sequencer packages include sophisticated score-writing facilities which enable you to print out sheet music for your compositions, in which case you'll need a printer which is compatible both with your computer and the software package. However, some musical literacy is useful because the computer doesn't always interpret what you play in the same way that a trained score writer would.

sequencer set-up

In a typical set-up, a MIDI master keyboard is connected to a sequencer via a MIDI cable so that when the sequencer is set to record, any notes played on the keyboard are recorded as MIDI data, and like the multitrack tape machine, a sequencer has multiple tracks into which to record the various musical parts of your composition. You might have 16 MIDI tracks set up so that each is on a different MIDI channel for use with a 16-part multitimbral module enabling you to play back all 16 tracks at once. But if you only have an 8-part multitimbral module, then you can only play back eight different musical parts at once, regardless of how many tracks your sequencer has.

It would be tedious having to change the MIDI channel on which your master keyboard transmits every time you wanted to record a new track so modern sequencers invariably convert the incoming MIDI data to the appropriate channel for you. This way, once a track is finished, you simply move on to the next one and keep playing with the new sound.

sequence editing

In many ways, a MIDI sequencer is like a word processor – you can delete or replace wrong musical notes, you can use the same phrase more than once by copying it or you can move sections about. In some ways, a better analogy might be the 'player piano' or pianola, where a punched paper roll holds the instructions that make the piano play, except in the case of MIDI you have a multitrack, virtual 'paper roll' capable of controlling many instruments at the same time.

By entering edit mode, you can change the value, timing and velocity of any note or even build up entire compositions by entering the notes manually. A number of editing options are usually available including the ability to transpose your music, either as you play or after recording, and you have the ability to make the music louder or softer by adjusting the overall note velocity values.

On some systems you can even compress the dynamic range of your MIDI data to even out the difference between your louder notes and the softer ones and delay or advance tracks relative to each other. This is frequently achieved by recalculating the note data during playback, but the real data isn't changed so you can always revert to your original performance data.

quantisation

One important feature common to both hardware and software sequencers is the ability to quantise data after recording. When you quantise something, the timing is changed so as to push each note you've recorded to the nearest exact subdivision of a bar. For example, if you are working in 4/4 time and you select 16 as your quantise value, everything moves so as to fall on the nearest 16th of a bar. Overquantising will ruin the feel of some types of music, but in dance music where precise timing is essential, the quantise feature is routinely used.

A sequencer will record just about any MIDI data you send it (with the exception of MIDI clock), and unless you deliberately filter out certain types of MIDI data, you can record Note On/Off, Pitch, Velocity, Aftertouch and Controller information as well as MIDI Program Changes and even System Exclusive data which is what you get if you do a patch dump from your instrument.

A MIDI Program Change recorded during the count-in period of a track will ensure that the connected synth switches to the correct patch before playing commences, and when your sequence is played back, the sequencer transmits the MIDI information to the receiving synth in exactly the same order and with the same timing as you originally played it. Because MIDI is only data, you can change the tempo after recording without affecting the pitch (unlike a tape recorder where you're dealing with sound rather than MIDI data).

sequencer types

MIDI sequencers are all really computer technology, but you can choose a software-based system that runs on a desktop PC such as an Apple Mac, Apple Power Mac, IBM PC or Atari, or instead you can go for a one-box, dedicated solution where everything you need is in one portable package. The main difference between the two types is the way in which the recorded information is displayed as the hardware models don't have the benefit of a large computer screen.

Whichever type you use, it is very important to save your work to disk at regular intervals. Most hardware sequencers have a built-in disk drive, allowing songs to be saved as files on floppy disk, though some models use battery-backed-up memory instead of disks.

midi interface

Unless you're using an Atari ST which has an integral MIDI interface, you'll need to buy an external MIDI interface unless one of your synths or modules has a computer interface built in. A basic sequencing set-up is shown in Figure 9.3. This shows a MIDI master keyboard, but if you are using a synth as a master keyboard, select Local Off on the master keyboard and connect the MIDI In of your master synth to one of the outputs of your MIDI Thru box.

As the record and playback controls of a typical sequencer are designed to look similar to tape recorder transport buttons, there will be a means to examine your stored MIDI data and make changes to it if necessary.

midi troubleshooting

In a typical MIDI system, the MIDI data originates at the master keyboard which is connected via its MIDI Out to the MIDI In of your sequencer. As mentioned earlier, if your keyboard includes a synth section, then turn Local Off and patch a MIDI cable from the sequencer's MIDI Out (or from your

Master keyboard should be set to Local Off mode to prevent creating a MIDI feedback loop. If no Local On/Off facility is provided, set master keyboard to transmit on MIDI channel 1 and set sequencer Thru to Off on channel 1

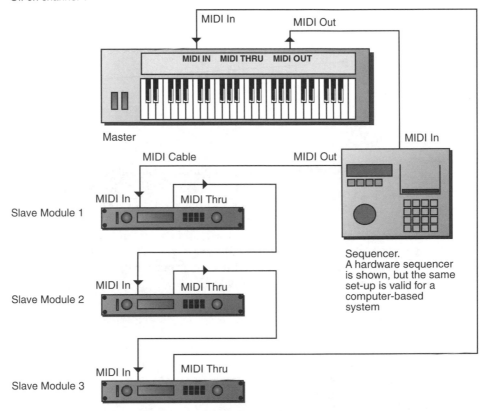

Figure 9.3: Basic sequencing system

Thru box) to the keyboard's MIDI In. Up to three modules can normally be chained from Thru to In without problems, but longer chains may suffer stuck or missed notes as mentioned earlier. If you have more than three MIDI devices, a Thru box is highly recommended.

If you've connected up your system as described but no sound comes out, here are a few things to check:

★ Make sure your amplification system and all your MIDI units are switched on and the volumes turned up to a reasonable level.

★ Ensure that your synth modules are set to Multi or Sequencer mode as appropriate.

★ Check your MIDI cable connections. If one of the modules has a combined MIDI Out/Thru socket, ensure MIDI Thru is enabled. Most sequencers have an indicator to show that they are receiving MIDI data.

★ Check the MIDI channels on your modules. If two or more instruments play the same part, check whether more than one module is set to the same MIDI channel or perhaps something's still in Omni mode.

★ If your master keyboard plays its own sounds when you're trying to record using another module, check that Local Off is turned Off.

★ If playing a single note results in a burst of notes, if you get stuck notes or if the polyphony seems less than it should be, you probably have a MIDI loop where data generated by the master keyboard is passing through the sequencer and getting back to the input of the master keyboard. Here it goes around the system again and again, choking the system with unnecessary and unwanted data. This usually happens when you have a keyboard synth as your master keyboard and Local Off is accidentally switched to Local On.

midi sound sources

MIDI sequencers can be used to control synthesizers, MIDI electronic pianos or organs, samplers or drum machines, but there is a limit to the number of notes that a sound module or synthesizer can play at once, and this is known as the maximum polyphony. If you try to play more notes than this, then one of the notes already sounding will be cut off. In a multitimbral instrument, the polyphony is shared between the various instruments so that if, for example, the piano isn't playing, the string part can use more notes before the polyphony runs out. Different instruments have different systems for sharing their polyphony but you'll need to look in your instrument handbooks to find out how your own instrument behaves.

drum machines

Technically speaking, drum machines are also synthesizers of a sort – they are simply MIDI modules with their own rhythm sequencer built in. The drum sounds may be played over MIDI exactly like conventional synth notes, but instead of each key giving you a new pitch of the same drum sound, drum machines are organised so that you get a different drum sound for each key played. A drum machine with no internal rhythm sequencer is known as a drum module. Most people who use drum machines with sequencers ignore the drum machine's internal sequencer and instead use the drum machine in the same way as any other sound module. New drum parts are then recorded directly from the keyboard, usually in two or three passes to make things simpler.

samplers

A MIDI sampler is very similar to a synthesizer, expect that instead of having built-in sounds, you can record your own sounds and then play them back at any pitch. The sounds might be musical instruments, but you can also turn household objects, such as pans or bottles, into new instruments. For example, tap a bottle, sample it, then play it back at different pitches from the keyboard and you have your own xylophone. Libraries of ready made sample sounds are available on both CD and CD-ROM.

midi connections

Earlier we learned that MIDI instruments have three MIDI sockets, labelled In, Out and Thru, though some models actually have a combined MIDI Out and Thru connection. The master instrument in a system always sends information from its MIDI Out socket, which is connected to the MIDI In socket of the first slave, and if you want a longer chain, I've already explained that you can take the MIDI Thru of the slave and connect it to the MIDI In of the next slave. However, you can't chain instruments together indefinitely, because the MIDI signal gets slightly distorted every time it passes through another unit and, eventually, there comes a point where the system becomes unreliable and some of the slaves start missing notes or, worse still, playing notes and forgetting to turn them off again!

midi thru box

Unless you have a very simple MIDI system, you should use a MIDI Thru box as shown in Figure 9.4. This is fed from the MIDI Out of the sequencer and has several MIDI Thru outputs, each of which can be connected to a different MIDI slave module.

You may have noticed so far that the only MIDI Out that's been used is on the master synth or keyboard – the MIDI Outs of the slave units have been left unconnected. The reason modules have MIDI Outs is that if they are being edited via software and a computer with a MIDI interface, the MIDI Out is required to transfer information about the module and the sounds it contains back to the computer.

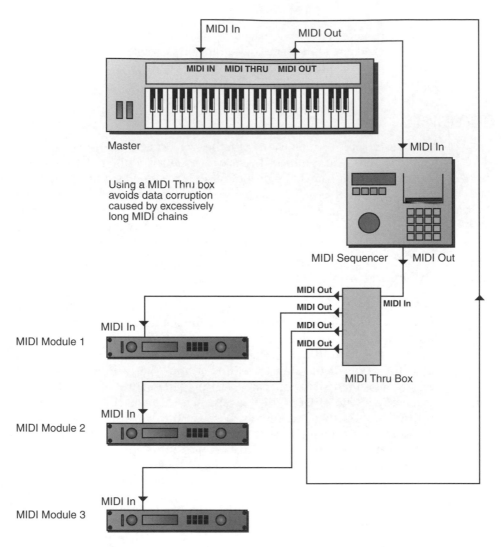

midi program change

There's a great deal more useful information than can be transmitted over MIDI than musical notes. Most MIDI synthesizers are programmable, and have the ability to store a great number of different sounds, which can be recalled almost instantly. One way to recall sounds is to use the front panel buttons, but you can also do it over MIDI. MIDI provides direct access for up to 128 sound patches, and when you change the patch on your master keyboard using the front panel controls, a Program Change command is transmitted from the MIDI Out (unless this function has deliberately been disabled via a software option). Program change messages may also be used to select the effects patches on a MIDI effects unit or to switch drum kits on a drum sound module.

bank change messages

Some MIDI instruments provide far more than 128 different sounds, in which case these have to be stored in banks where each bank contains up to 128 different patches or programs. MIDI bank change commands may then be sent to switch from one bank to another, though at the moment, there are several non-standard bank change message formats so you may need to consult the manual that came with your module.

real time control

There's more to playing a synthesizer than simply hitting the right notes on the keyboard – there are performance controls such as the pitch bend and mod wheels which add interest and life to a performance. As you might imagine, the effect of moving these wheels may also be transmitted over MIDI.

MIDI instruments can often be 'scaled' so that the maximum travel of the pitch bend wheel causes a pitch shift anywhere between one semitone or a full octave in either direction from a spring-loaded centre position. Most people use a default setting of two semitones for full travel of the wheel, but whatever scale you choose, it is important that any instruments likely to play at the same time are set with the same scaling values. The same is true when you're working with a sequencer, and it's generally advisable to set up all your instruments to the same pitch bend range.

midi volume

On a master instrument that sends master volume information, turning up the master volume slider will send the appropriate control information over MIDI and the receiving instrument will respond to it. Some older instruments do not respond to MIDI volume control, but most modern instruments do.

midi controllers

If you look in the manual for your synthesizer or module, you'll also find that a number of other performance controls are supported by MIDI including sustain pedals, joysticks, sostenuto, pan and many more. These so-called MIDI controllers are divided into two main types: those that are either on or off, and those that can be varied in fine increments. The latter are known as Continuous Controllers. A sustain pedal has a simple on/off function whereas pan or volume are continuous controllers. Most things in MIDI, including controllers, have a maximum value of 128, which equates to a 7-bit message in computer terms.

midi modes

As stipulated at the start of this chapter, the majority of MIDI instruments can be set to work on any of the 16 MIDI channels and I mentioned that there is also an Omni mode, which allows the unit to respond to all incoming data, regardless of channel. It is also possible to tell an instrument whether to play polyphonically or monophonically, and while polyphonic operation is the most common, mono operation has certain applications when playing bass lines, analogue-style lead lines, or for use with guitar synths where each string transmits on its own MIDI channel and needs to be allocated, in effect, its own monophonic synthesizer to work properly.

The four possible combinations of Omni On/Off and Poly/Mono are known as the four MIDI modes and they are defined as:

Mode 1: Omni On/Poly
Mode 2: Omni On/Mono
Mode 3: Omni Off/Poly
Mode 4: Omni Off/Mono

Mode 1 allows the instrument to play polyphonically but it will attempt to play all incoming data, regardless of the channel it was sent on.

Mode 2 is widely held to be a mistake and I can't recall anyone finding a valid use for it. Many instruments don't include Mode 2 for that reason.

Mode 3 is the most common mode as it allows the instrument to respond to individual MIDI channels and to play polyphonically.

Mode 4 turns a multitimbral synth into several monophonic synths, each on its own MIDI channel. Mode 4 is used mainly when playing mono-style melody or bass lines for use with guitar synths.

midi and tempo

Drum machines have in-built sequencers allowing them to create and play back drum patterns at different tempos. Drum machines (and MIDI sequencers) both send and receive MIDI Clock, which is like a series of metronome pulses, but instead of getting four to the bar, you get 96 per quarter note or 384 pulses per 4/4 bar. These pulses do much the same job as the sprocket holes used to guide cine film through the projector – they keep it in sync.

MIDI Clock makes it possible to sync two or more MIDI devices together where one device is again the master and the other the slave. This way, you can connect two drum machines so that they both run together at precisely the same tempo, or you can slave a sequencer to a drum machine or vice versa. Even when the master machine is not playing, it is still sending out MIDI Clock at the current tempo, which means that any connected slave device knows exactly what tempo to start at when it receives a Start command. The MIDI commands for starting and stopping drum machines and sequencers are known as MIDI Real Time messages.

real time midi

The Stop command will cause both the master and slave machines to stop

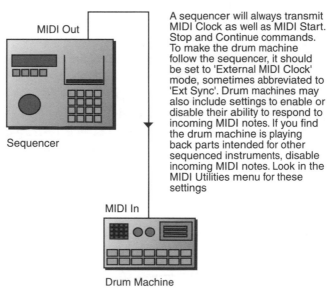

MIDI Out

Sequencer

A sequencer will always transmit MIDI Clock as well as MIDI Start. Stop and Continue commands. To make the drum machine follow the sequencer, it should be set to 'External MIDI Clock' mode, sometimes abbreviated to 'Ext Sync'. Drum machines may also include settings to enable or disable their ability to respond to incoming MIDI notes. If you find the drum machine is playing back parts intended for other sequenced instruments, disable incoming MIDI notes. Look in the MIDI Utilities menu for these settings

MIDI In

Drum Machine

Figure 9.5: MIDI Clock sync

running while a Continue command forces the machines to continue playing from the point at which they were stopped. A Start message always forces the master and slave to start from the beginning of the song. The master slave is always switched to its internal clock mode while the slave machine must be switched to external clock mode. Figure 9.5 shows how a MIDI master/slave system is linked for clock sync.

sequencer syncing

MIDI instruments provide a huge range of sounds and MIDI sequencers let you record and replay multitrack compositions involving lots of instruments, but you can't record audio onto a conventional MIDI sequencer. If you want to have both audio and MIDI controlled sounds in a mix, and you don't have a sequencer with an integral hard disk audio recording system, you need a means of getting your tape recorder and your sequencer working as a team.

You could create a complete backing track using your sequencer and your synths, samplers and drum machines, then mix this onto your multitrack tape machine leaving two tracks free for vocals or acoustic instruments, but there's a better way to work. All that's needed is some way to get the sequencer running in sync with your Multitracker and you have the best of both worlds. Working this way, all the sequenced sounds can run directly into the final mix in perfect sync with the vocals or acoustic sounds recorded on tape. And because your synth sounds are never recorded onto multitrack, the sound quality is limited only by the type of mastering machine you use. But how can you sync your sequencer to your tape machine?

midi sync

Both sequencers and drum machines can be synchronised to tape recorders, and the normal way to do this is to have the tape recorder working as a master and the drum machine or sequencer as a slave. Because tape machines don't output MIDI directly, an interface box or sync unit is needed to enable the MIDI timing data to be recorded onto one track of the tape. However there are several possible systems, the main points of which are summarised below.

simple fsk

This system requires a MIDI Clock-to-tape sync box and works by recording a timing track derived from MIDI Clock onto one of the multitrack machine, usually onto the highest numbered track. When the

tape is relayed, this information starts the sequencer and sends it MIDI
Clock timing pulses to keep it synchronised. Such systems are tedious to
use because every time the tape is stopped part way through a song, it
has to be started from the beginning again to restore sync.

smart fsk

Smart FSK is similar to the above, but it works with another piece of
hidden MIDI information known as MIDI Song Position Pointers or SPPs.
Most modern equipment generates and recognises these and everything
is transparent to the user – there's no set-up to worry about. Providing
your sync box uses Smart FSK, you can start the tape anywhere in the
song and the sequencer will lock up within a couple of seconds.

A big advantage of MIDI Clock-based sync systems is that the tempo of the
music is contained within the sync code so any tempo changes in the
original sequence will be followed faithfully and automatically when the
tape is run.

Smart FSK Tape-to-MIDI Sync boxes with in-built MIDI merge facilities are
best because this allows new sequencer parts to be recorded while the
sequencer is synced to tape. Figure 9.6 shows how a Smart FSK box is
connected.

smpte

SMPTE is a professional time code borrowed from the film industry and is
unnecessarily complicated for syncing MIDI sequencers to tape machines.
However, some MIDI sequencers have dedicated SMPTE sync boxes that
are still easy to use because the sequencer program looks after tempo
mapping automatically. If you have such a sequencer, SMPTE sync is worth
considering, though MTC is a more popular standard for contemporary
equipment.

SMPTE code contains only elapsed time information which is subdivided into
hours, minutes, seconds and frames of film or TV picture, so a conversion has
to be done to calculate the tempo. Tempo information, including any tempo
changes, must be stored in a tempo map which is usually stored as part of the
MIDI sequence. If this is handled by your sequencer, it's all quite
straightforward, but if not, Smart FSK is a lot simpler. SMPTE comes in several
frame formats depending on whether it is being used for film or television.
The most popular formats are 30fps for US TV, 25fps for European TV and
24fps for film. The format is usually selectable in software, and if you're not
doing film or TV work, the local TV frame rate is normally adopted.

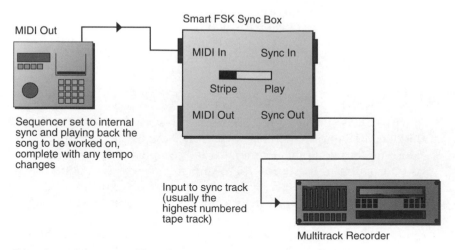

MIDI Out

Sequencer set to internal sync and playing back the song to be worked on, complete with any tempo changes

Input to sync track (usually the highest numbered tape track)

Setup for striping tape with code

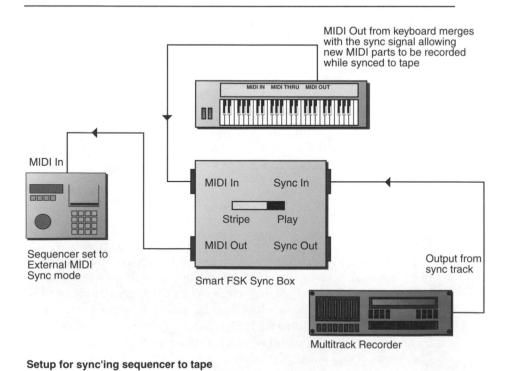

MIDI Out from keyboard merges with the sync signal allowing new MIDI parts to be recorded while synced to tape

MIDI In

Sequencer set to External MIDI Sync mode

Output from sync track

Setup for sync'ing sequencer to tape

Figure 9.6: Connecting a Smart FSK sync box

mtc

MTC or MIDI Time Code, is the direct MIDI equivalent of SMPTE and most modern sequencers read and generate it. MTC contains the same embedded timing information as SMPTE, including the choice of frame rates, but once again, if your sequencer doesn't handle the tempo maps for you, Smart FSK is still a simpler option. The majority of modern sequencers, however, support MTC automatically, making it a very practical option. To use MTC with tape, an MTC-to-tape sync interface box is required. Many of the larger multiport MIDI interfaces include full SMPTE and MTC support.

general midi

General MIDI is another stage of standardisation which has been added to the existing MIDI protocol to enable manufacturers to build synthesizers and synth modules that exhibit a specified degree of compatibility in certain areas. General MIDI sets out strict rules for patch mapping, drum note mapping, multitimbrality and polyphony, and the aim is to allow a MIDI sequence recorded using one GM module to be played back on any other GM module without the need to remap patches, move drum note allocations or worry about running out of parts or polyphony. This doesn't mean that all GM synths have to sound exactly the same, but it does mean that, for example, a piano preset on one machine must be in the same patch location as a similar piano preset on any other GM machine.

pre gm compatibility

Sequencer users often insert patch change commands at the start of the piece, and at any subsequent locations in the piece where a sound is required to change. That way, whenever you play back the sequence through the same instruments and modules, the correct sounds will automatically be called up. However, if you were to play the sequence back on a friend's MIDI system, you may well find that all the sounds are completely wrong because the patches are not only completely different in sound, but any that are suitable are also stored in different patch locations. In the case of programmable instruments, this kind of chaos is difficult to avoid because most users have their own system for storing their edited sounds. Furthermore, the factory presets that come with most MIDI instruments were not stored in any particular order prior to the introduction of GM.

Another potential stumbling block is the drum and percussion part. Is your friend's system set up with the drum part on the same MIDI channel and, if so, are the drum sounds mapped to the same notes?

Let's say you're lucky and you get all the sounds mapped out. There's still a good chance you'll come unstuck when it comes to controller information; perhaps one of the modules doesn't respond to Controller 7 (Master Volume), or perhaps the pitch bend ranges are set differently to those on your own system.

general midi philosophy

General MIDI was devised for use in situations where a high degree of compatibility is essential, for example when replaying pre-recorded MIDI song files. Using GM, musicians can play each other's GM song files and be confident that they will sound more or less the way they should, even though there are subtle subjective differences between one manufacturer's GM machine and another. This has opened up the market for commercially available MIDI song files, and though these hold little attraction for the serious composer, they are very effective as live backings and may also be used to gain recording, mixing and effects processing experience.

polyphony and multitimbrality

The problem with polyphony and multitimbrality is that you can never have enough of it! GM instruments provide the ability to play back 16 parts on 16 MIDI channels with a minimum of 24-note polyphony. However, where a synth uses two voices to make up a sound, the actual polyphony is further reduced, which means that a GM song file written for one GM machine could still come unstuck if played back using a different GM module where the manufacturers claim that number of voices and polyphony mean the same thing.

roland's gs format

Much of the present GM format owes its existence to Roland's own protocols, so it's hardly surprising that Roland have gone one step further and devised an enhanced version of General MIDI which they call GS. Realising that many users wouldn't be satisfied with 128 preset sounds, Roland have designed their GS machines to offer several alternative banks of sounds, the basic GM set (Capital Tones) being the first bank (Bank 0). There are up to seven 'Variation Tones' based on each of the Capital Tones and these are arranged so as to have the same program change numbers as the tones from which they are derived. In other words, all the variation tones of a Piano Capital Tone will still be pianos, though they will all be subtly different. Further banks are provided for sounds known as Sub-Capital Tones, which are less obviously related to the Capital Tones.

A Bank Change (in Roland's case based on Controller 0) allows the user to switch between the various banks. Conventional program change commands are then used to select the sounds within each bank – a neat way to get around MIDI's limitation of being able to directly address only 128 patches. Yamaha have their own extended GM system, which they call XG. The major difference, as far as the user is concerned, is that Yamaha's XG system uses different bank change commands to GS. At the time of writing, GS looks set to remain the adopted standard.

general midi overview

General MIDI aims to define a minimum set of MIDI capabilities with which all GM MIDI devices must comply. The main points are as follows:

★ A GM instrument must support all 16 MIDI channels simultaneously to provide 16-part multitimbrality.

★ Percussion parts must be on MIDI channel 10, a minimum set of 47 standard sound types, including the most common drum and latin percussion sounds, must be provided and these must all be mapped in accordance with the GM standard. This mapping owes a lot to Roland's original mapping system.

★ GM instruments must be capable of 24-note polyphony and notes must be allocated dynamically. However, the specification allows eight notes to be reserved for percussion, leaving 16 for the other instruments.

★ All 128 preset sounds are defined as to their type and patch location. Though there is some variation in sound between one module and another, the instrument type (and even playing style in the case of basses, for example) for each patch location is quite rigidly defined, right down to the dog barks and gun shots in the special effects section. Some of the sounds, such as pads, are a little more flexible but they must still be of a roughly similar tone and style.

★ All GM instruments must respond to the same set of MIDI Controllers. The MIDI Controller implementation includes the ability to change the

master tuning and pitch bend wheel range via MIDI, Reset All
Controllers (which resets all MIDI Controllers to their default values),
and All Notes Off. All GM machines must also respond to Pitch Bend
and Aftertouch.

chapter 10

using a sub mixer

Cassette multitrackers are a useful compromise between flexibility and cost, and for better audio quality, MiniDisc and hard disk alternatives are available. But unless your requirements are fairly modest, you'll eventually run out of input channels. For example, if you plan to work with a MIDI system, or need the flexibility to handle multi-mic recording sessions, you'll need a large number of input channels, either for recording or for mixing. One cost-effective way around this is to add an external mixer which can handle the appropriate number of microphones or MIDI instruments.

track outputs

If you have a large MIDI system, the external mixer may be used to combine the outputs from the various MIDI modules down to stereo, then the stereo output of the mixer can be plugged into two spare input channels of your multitracker, or even into a pair of aux returns to be added to the off-tape mix. Alternatively, the multitracker outputs can feed two channels of your external mixer as shown in Figure 10.1.

Better still, if your multitracker has separate track outputs, you can feed each of these into channels of your external mixer so as to make use of the better facilities external mixers invariably have to offer.

A useful tip if you're syncing to MIDI and don't have separate track outputs is to pan tracks 1 and 2 hard left and right respectively, then pull down the fader on track 3 and use the pre-fade (Foldback) aux send to route channel 3 to the Foldback output jack. Now you have three separate outputs; track 1 is on the Left buss, track 2 is on the Right buss and track 3 is on the Foldback output jack. These can be fed to three mixer channels for external mixing. Track 4 will contain time code, and this has its own output on all but the most rudimentary multitrackers.

You could simply record the 'MIDI mix' onto a pair of tracks in your multitrack recording, but a great many musicians prefer to sync their MIDI sequencer to the multitracker so as to bypass the need to record the MIDI

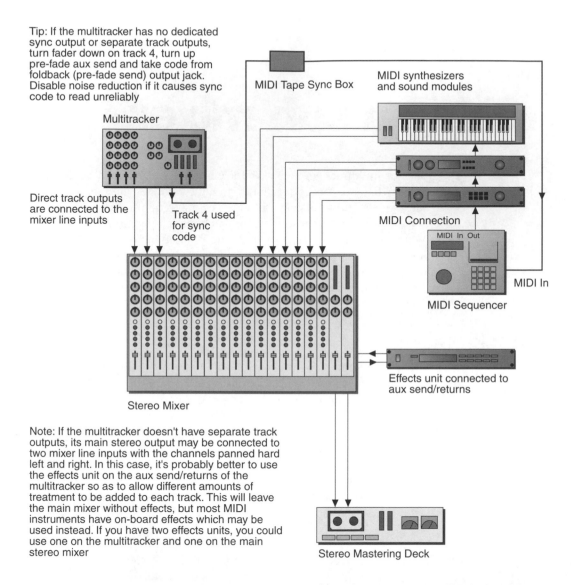

Tip: If the multitracker has no dedicated sync output or separate track outputs, turn fader down on track 4, turn up pre-fade aux send and take code from foldback (pre-fade send) output jack. Disable noise reduction if it causes sync code to read unreliably

MIDI Tape Sync Box

MIDI synthesizers and sound modules

Multitracker

Direct track outputs are connected to the mixer line inputs

Track 4 used for sync code

MIDI Connection

MIDI In Out

MIDI Sequencer

MIDI In

Stereo Mixer

Effects unit connected to aux send/returns

Note: If the multitracker doesn't have separate track outputs, its main stereo output may be connected to two mixer line inputs with the channels panned hard left and right. In this case, it's probably better to use the effects unit on the aux send/returns of the multitracker so as to allow different amounts of treatment to be added to each track. This will leave the main mixer without effects, but most MIDI instruments have on-board effects which may be used instead. If you have two effects units, you could use one on the multitracker and one on the main stereo mixer

Stereo Mastering Deck

Figure 10.1: Mixing multitracker and MIDI instruments

instruments onto multitrack tape at all. In this case, the MIDI contribution to the mix runs 'live' as you mix and is combined with the recorded tracks from tape. Admittedly you lose one tape track for recording the time code necessary to sync the audio and MIDI, but the benefit of having separate control over all the MIDI instruments outweighs this disadvantage. Because the sequencer is synced to the tape machine, the two parts always run in perfect time with each other.

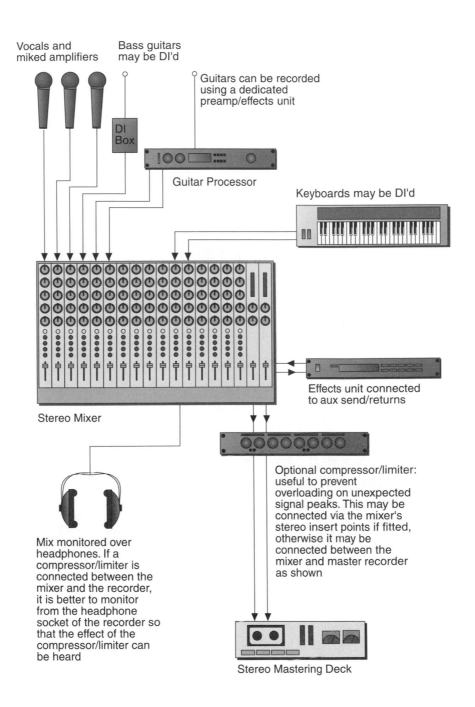

Vocals and
miked amplifiers

Bass guitars
may be DI'd

Guitars can be recorded
using a dedicated
preamp/effects unit

DI
Box

Guitar Processor

Keyboards may be DI'd

Effects unit connected
to aux send/returns

Stereo Mixer

Mix monitored over
headphones. If a
compressor/limiter is
connected between the
mixer and the recorder,
it is better to monitor
from the headphone
socket of the recorder so
that the effect of the
compressor/limiter can
be heard

Optional compressor/limiter:
useful to prevent
overloading on unexpected
signal peaks. This may be
connected via the mixer's
stereo insert points if fitted,
otherwise it may be
connected between the
mixer and master recorder
as shown

Stereo Mastering Deck

Figure 10.2: Live recording using a stereo mixer

live recording

For live recording, a simple stereo mixer can be used to mix a number of mics into stereo to be recorded onto two tracks of your multitracker while the remaining two tracks are used conventionally to record, for example, the lead vocal and the lead guitar. Figure 10.2 shows the use of a simple stereo mixer in live recording.

chapter 11

the recording session

Before you start work, you need to make sure you have something worth recording, and because the project studio owner is more often than not recording his or her own material, this means having good songs, rehearsing them thoroughly, and making sure that all your instruments play properly and stay in tune.

Step one is to make sure you have some good material to record, and if you play live on a regular basis, you must have a fair idea of which songs go down best with your audience. Even so, on some numbers it may just be your visual stage act that gets the applause – on tape, you can only be heard, not seen, so your preparations should start right back in the rehearsal room. When you're working on songs, it's a good idea to tape absolutely everything to help you to spot weaknesses more effectively. By the same token, if you're thinking of recording an unfamiliar band in your home studio, make sure they send you a tape first.

Another advantage of making rough recordings is that you'll be able to see if there's anything about the arrangement that doesn't quite work on record. Solos might need shortening, intros and links might need cutting down – if something isn't in there for a reason, shorten it or cut it out altogether. It usually helps if you play the tapes to a friend who isn't as familiar with the material as you are – you'll learn a lot from his reaction.

fine tuning

After sorting out the arrangements, you need to rehearse – every detail must be correct or the mistakes will stick out like a sore thumb. What's more, you often need to learn the song well enough so you can play it without the vocals or the guitar solo, because vocals and guitar are usually added afterwards.

Even if you have rehearsed your parts and feel confident of performing well for the microphone, poor tuning and timing can still let you down. When working on pop music that incorporates sequenced MIDI tracks, it is common practice to play along with a click track when recording, and I know some drummers find this particularly difficult to get used to. If this is a problem, it helps to have the drummer play along to a drum machine for practice, before the recording session.

If you're working on a pop or dance track and using a MIDI sequencer, consider using some sequenced drums and some live. For example, you could program the bass drum and snare to get a really tight feel, then overdub live toms and hi-hats to put the humanity back into it. This is often done on rock recording as well as on pop music.

tuning blues

Guitars should be fitted with new strings before a session, ideally the night before, and the instrument should be taken out of its case and allowed to acclimatise for as long as possible before tuning up. Take just two or three turns of the string around the tuning peg and give all the strings a good pull to make sure there is no stretch left in them. That way you shouldn't have tuning problems, even with freshly changed strings. However, use an electronic guitar tuner to check every instrument is in tune before every take and every overdub. Tuning has a habit of drifting as the temperature or humidity changes, and if your instrument has intonation problems or rogue buzzes, get it sorted out before attempting to record.

drum tuning

A certain amount of expertise and experience is needed to tune a drum kit for the studio, but a good drum sound starts with a kit that's in good condition. Worn heads produce a dreadful sound that no amount of trying to 'fix it in the mix' will put right, and if you don't have particularly good cymbals, borrow or hire some. Watch out for rattling fittings and squeaking stools or pedals and fix these before the session – it helps to keep a can of WD40 handy to cure squeaks.

A final tip on drum tuning is not to overdamp them. Some people stick so much tape on a drum, it sounds like hitting a suitcase, but most of the ring will get lost in the mix; err on the side of minimal damping using small pads of tissue or cloth and tape.

session planning

How long should you allow if you're recording an outside band rather than your own material? How much you can get done in a day depends on the proficiency of the artistes, the complexity of the music and whether you're producing demos or masters. For example, you wouldn't normally expect to get more than three or four demo tracks finished in one day, whereas a well recorded single could take you several days to perfect. Even for demo work, allow a couple of hours for getting all the mics set up and for getting the basic sound right. You'll also need time to mix, which could be anything from half an hour per song for a simple demo, to a day or more for a single or album track.

For analogue open reel or cassette tape machines, clean the heads with a cotton bud dipped in isopropyl alcohol at the start of each session, and again after every three or four hours. Always use good quality, new tape. Anything else is false economy.

This method of cleaning applies only to traditional analogue recorders – digital tape machines have special cleaning tapes while tapeless systems based on computer-style hard disk drives require no cleaning at all. Similarly, make sure that your instruments are working properly and that you aren't plagued with faulty leads or mysterious hums and buzzes. Fit new strings to any guitars being used and ensure that drum heads are in good condition. If this sounds obvious, you'd be surprised at how many people turn up for professional recording sessions with instruments that are virtually unplayable through lack of basic maintenance.

monitoring

Though some vocalists have problems working with headphones, it's something they'll have to learn to live with if they want to make records. It is important to minimise the amount of sound leakage from the headphones to the vocal mic, so enclosed headphones are preferred. Vocalists in particular often benefit from having reverb added to the headphone mix as it encourages a good performance and generally makes them feel more relaxed.

recording order

In a typical pop mix, it's quite common to record at least the bass, drums and guitar at the same time as it helps to maintain the feel of musicians playing together. This forms the basic backing track over which additional instrumentation and vocals can be overdubbed. Because there are no vocals recorded at this stage, it can help to have the singer record a rough guide vocal part onto a spare track of tape, but if you have no tracks to spare, have the singer use a mic and sing along into the headphone monitoring system so that everyone knows where they are. Most people play better if there's a guide vocal to listen to, even if they can find their way through the song without it.

On stage, it's quite normal for a guitarist in a one-guitar band to stop playing chords and go into a solo, but in the studio, you can always hear where the rhythm stops playing. It's usually better to record the rhythm part all the way through the song, including the solo section when you first put down the backing track, then add the solo as a separate overdub. This also provides more chance for getting the solo just right. Make sure you know exactly when the solo will end, and get the singer to dictate cues on the guide track if need be.

If you're recording a vocal or acoustic instrument part that may need patching up with a few punch-ins, ask the players to stay where they are after they have finished recording. If they come out to listen to the recording, the chances are they'll never return to exactly the same position relative to the microphone, and you'll probably hear a slight change in level or tone whenever you punch in.

keeping records

Always make a chart or track sheet of what instruments will be recorded on what tracks, otherwise you might get half way through a song and find you've run out of tracks. This is particularly important if you're working with only four or eight tracks as you'll almost certainly have to bounce something to make everything fit. If the song needs an intro that will be recorded after the main backing track has gone down, get the drummer to record the correct number of bars of clicks. For example, if you need a 16-bar intro, record a 17-bar click count-in.

demos

If you're doing demos, don't spend too much time overproducing them. If they're too fussy, it makes it more difficult for an A&R man to visualise alternative ways of approaching the song. If the vocal is well sung and you have a good melody, you're more than half way to a good demo.

getting the sounds

When doing a sound check, only the musician whose sound you are working on should play. If everyone insists on playing all the time, you'll waste a lot of time, your patience will become worn, and you'll probably end up with a less than ideal sound. Hide the drummer's sticks if you have to!

counting in

A tip is to get the drummer to count in each song by tapping out the first three beats of the count-in on the hi-hat, leaving the fourth beat silent. This way, when you come to tidy up the start of the song at the mix, it'll be a lot easier to get a clean run into the first beat.

When you get around to the actual recording, everybody will probably be a little excited, but remind them to stay dead silent during the count-in, and more importantly, at the end of each song. Many a perfect ending has been spoiled by somebody yelling 'Yeah, that's the one!' over the decay of the final chord, or by the drummer dumping his sticks on his kit. Wait a good ten seconds until all sound has ceased before you even breathe! Similarly, make sure you have no unduly noisy clothing or jewellery – you'd be surprised what finds its way into the mic.

Be ruthless about tuning and double check guitars and basses before every take; even the best guitars have a habit of drifting out of pitch as the room warms up. Modern keyboards don't have this problem, but old analogue synths should be switched on at least an hour before you start to record, and even then, check them at regular intervals. If you don't already have an electronic tuner, buy one!

track discipline

Most project studios are based around 4- or 8-track systems, which doesn't leave a lot of leeway for bouncing. To save wasting tracks, any live band recordings should be done with most if not all the members playing together, and you might find it helpful to put down a guide vocal as you play.

Instrumental solos, lead vocals and backing vocals can be added later so that you get as many takes as you need to get them right, and because of the level disparity, acoustic instruments should also be overdubbed.

Because solos often come in between vocal verses, you can sometimes get away with recording your solo on the vocal track. You just have to be careful to drop out of record before the vocals come back in, otherwise you'll wipe over them.

If you have to bounce any tracks during the course of the session, try to bounce things that aren't main components of the mix. For example, you can usually get away with bouncing backing vocals or pad keyboard parts, but bouncing drums or main vocals is to be avoided where possible. If you do have to bounce an important part, try to do so no more than once, and consider adding a hint of top boost as you bounce to make up for any clarity lost in the process.

no second best

Don't let any mistakes get by, either musical or technical – I've said this before on numerous occasions, but it really is very important to understand that you can't just 'fix it in the mix'. No matter how many effects or sound effects you heap on a mistake, you'll still hear it, so do what you have to do and replace any substandard work before you even think about mixing. Listen to your recordings for bad notes, bad timing, distortion and noises that shouldn't be there, such as clicking drum sticks or excessive guitar finger noise. Listening on headphones is generally the most revealing of such problems.

mixing

Mixing is the point in the proceedings where you get to balance the individual sounds you've recorded, modify their tonality, and add effects. For me, mixing is the most creative part of the whole process – it's where all your hard work comes together to produce the end result. While in professional circles there's invariably a producer looking over the engineer's shoulder calling the shots, most of us have to double as engineer and producer, and quite often as the artiste too, and that means we have to know something about music production as well as engineering.

A good mix starts with getting good sounds onto tape (or disk) in the first place – attempting to fix things in the mix really is an uphill struggle and rarely entirely successful.

No matter what system you're using for multitracking, you need to use the best possible mastering format so as to preserve your work to the highest possible quality. The most popular budget choice for use with cassette multitrackers is a good quality, hi-fi cassette deck, but for more serious work, DAT, DCC or Minidisc are significantly better. Good quality results may also be achieved by mixing onto a hi-fi video recorder as pointed out earlier in this book

before mixing

Once the recording stops and, ideally after a suitable break, the mixing session starts. At this point you should have track sheets describing what's on the various tape tracks, any notes taken during the recording, and all the mixer EQ, level and routing controls set to 'neutral' ready for a clean start. The only exception to this latter condition is if you've been setting up your mix as you record, in which case it's simply a matter of checking that nothing is routed that shouldn't be. If you have a separate mixer, ensure that if any channels are redundant that they're not routed either to the groups or the Left/Right buss. On channels where EQ will not be needed, bypass it, and mute any unused monitor inputs.

If you have a multitrack mixer with routing, it helps to separate logical groups of sounds into subgroups, so that the mix can be handled with fewer faders. For example, if the recording includes real drums, these are likely to occupy several tracks, so it makes sense to assign them to a single, stereo subgroup. Other candidates for subgrouping are backing vocals and multi-layered keyboard parts.

start in mono

I find it helpful to set up a balance in mono to start with so that you can see how well the separate sounds blend. Unless the quality of the original recording leaves something to be desired, it should be possible to set up a workable balance fairly quickly, without resorting to EQ. Don't worry about panning the sounds until a reasonably good balance has been achieved. Once a reasonable balance has been achieved, then you can think about adding EQ and effects. Whatever you do, don't get too bogged down trying to EQ individual tracks because they'll almost certainly sound quite different once the rest of the mix is up and running.

If MIDI instruments are to be a part of the mix, these may be fed into any spare input channels or even into spare aux returns, but if you don't have enough spare channels, then patching in a submixer is the best option. Sync signals should not be fed via the mixer because of the danger of crosstalk where high level sync codes are used. It is always best to use separate, external cables to route the time code track from the tape machine to the synchroniser.

setting a balance

On mixers with PFL buttons, the PFL metering system should be used for each input channel in turn to optimise the gain setting; the PFL meter should just go into the red on signal peaks. It is often easiest to balance the drums and bass first; once the rhythm section is working, add the lead vocal followed by the other parts of the mix, always being aware that you must leave space for the vocal. I invariably add some compression to vocals while mixing to even out the level, and if noise is in any way a problem, I'll also gate the vocals before the compressor. A useful compressor setting is to choose a fast attack combined with a release time of 0.5S or so and a ratio of between 4:1 and 12:1 depending on whether you want to hear the compressor working or not. If you're experiencing sibilance problems, try a less bright reverb setting or add a little EQ cut at around 6kHz.

panning

Once the mix starts to sound good in mono, you can work on the stereo panning. Bass drums, bass guitars and lead vocals should be left in the centre because these sounds carry most of the energy of a mix, and when reproduced over a stereo system, it's best to have both speakers sharing the load. Try not to monitor too loudly as this will affect your judgement and may eventually damage your hearing. The most logical monitoring level would be at the same level as the end user is likely to listen at – in other words, a sensible domestic listening volume.

Other instruments, backing vocals and effects can be spread out to create an illusion of space. Reverb should almost always be added in stereo as this gives the mix a sense of space and reality. Most digital reverberation units have a mono input and a stereo output. The ones with stereo inputs tend to use a mono mix of the left and right inputs to create the reverb, with only the original sound being passed through in stereo. This means that no matter where in the mix the original signal is panned, its reverb will come equally from both sides.

localisation

On the face of it, the fact that the reverb level is equal in the left and right channels tends to 'dilute' the effect of using panning to localise the original sound, but it helps when thinking through this type of situation to compare the outcome with what happens in a real life situation, such as when music is played in a concert hall. Take the example of a violin playing at one side of the stage; the direct sound will appear to come from the violin because our ears analyse the relative levels heard by the left and right ears and the phase relationship between these two sounds to establish direction. However, the room reverberation resulting from the performance will, essentially, come from everywhere at once because the sound is continually bouncing off all the hard surfaces in the room. In other words, we have a direct parallel to the digital reverb situation, in which the direct sound appears to come from whatever point we have panned it to in the mix, while the reverb comes from both sides. This does tend to dilute the stereo positioning of the original sound, but no more so than in real life.

Reverberant sound produces the illusion of space and depth, so the pragmatic way to look at it is that by adding reverb, you trade off a degree of stereo localisation for a sense of stereo space. Adding a short reverb to a panned mono sound is probably the most effective way of making it sound as though it exists in a natural environment.

performance panning

Very often we try to set up pan positions that correspond to the way in which performers might be arranged on a stage. This means placing the main vocals in the centre along with the bass guitar, bass drum and very often the snare drum too. The guitars and keyboards can be panned to either side, as can backing vocals, while the output from a stereo reverb unit is invariably panned to the left and right extremes.

If you are attempting to create the illusion of a live performance, there are pitfalls to be aware of. For example, it is very tempting to spread things out in the stereo mix simply because the opportunity is there, but this can lead to an unnatural, even uncomfortable sound; if you pan the various drums in a kit, or the high and low notes on a piano, hard left and right, you can end up with the illusion of a 30-foot wide instrument! The same is true of stereo keyboard synthesizers, and though it is tempting to spread them from ear to ear, it might be better to, for example, pan one side to the left or right extreme and the other to the centre of the mix. This will maintain some illusion of stereo spread but will confine it to just half of the soundstage.

Don't worry that you're not making full use of your stereo mixing capabilities simply because so many of your sounds are located at or near the centre of the mix. You only need to move a couple of sounds out to the sides to create a sense of space, and the addition of stereo reverb will greatly add to the sense of width.

perspective

Real music doesn't just exist along an imaginary line drawn from left to right, yet when we pan a sound between two loudspeakers, this is exactly what we are working with. The dimensions of height and depth are missing from the equation, so we have to simulate them using other techniques. Recent work has indicated that the early reflections produced when a sound occurs in an enclosed space have a profound influence on how near or far the sound appears to be from the listener. Intuitively, it seems logical that a more distant sound will contain a greater proportion of reverberant sound than a near one, but the spacing and rate of build-up of these reflections also appears to be important. If you have a reverb device which allows you to create early reflections patterns, it is worthwhile experimenting with the various options and making notes of any settings that produce a definite sense of closeness or distance. Small room or closely-spaced reflections patterns seem to create a sense of closeness or intimacy, but much more work has to be done in this area before we can dispense with trial and error.

stereo checklist

★ Pan bass instruments and bass drums to the centre of the mix. Snare drums tend also to work best when panned near the centre, but the toms and cymbals may be spread (not too widely) from left to right.

★ Keep the lead vocals close to the centre of the mix, as they are the focus of the performance, but experiment with positioning backing vocals to the sides.

★ When you pan an instrument away from the centre of the mix, don't always feel you have to set it hard left or right. Try to paint a picture, with your sounds spreading across the stereo stage in interesting ways and the main sounds nearest the centre.

★ Take care not to pan stereo mics or the outputs from a stereo instrument (such as a piano or drum kit) so wide as to produce the illusion of an instrument that is as wide as the stage!

★ Unless you are specifically trying to create a special effect, pan the outputs from your stereo reverb unit hard left and right and ensure they are at the same level in the mix.

★ Use your discretion when panning the outputs from stereo effects units such as delays and chorus units. Consider panning them over just half of the stereo soundstage – between dead centre and hard left for example.

problems?

Recording problems break down into many types, some clearly defined, others less so. The most obvious technical problems relate to things like noise, distortion, EQ and spill while the more artistic considerations include the wrong choice of sounds, poor timing, out of tune or just plain wrong notes.

Probably the most common technical problem is noise, which includes tape hiss, instrument amplifier hiss, amplifier hum and general digital noise from budget synths and effects units. You can attack noise on several different levels, and if the contamination is serious, you may need to use two or more of the following processes in combination.

A noise gate is a very effective way of removing noise during the pauses between sounds, and you'd be surprised how much you can clean up a mix by gating any channels containing parts that aren't playing all the way through the mix. For example, if the lead guitar solo only pops up in the middle of the song, you don't want any background noise on that track contributing to the mix the rest of the time, so bang a gate on it. It's also often worth gating vocals because there are usually pauses between words or phrases where nothing useful is happening. However, don't feel you have to gate out traces of breath noise, otherwise the vocal track may well end up sounding unnatural.

With any slowly decaying sounds, make sure you set an appropriately long gate release time. Even if some gated sounds appear to be slightly unnatural, there's a good chance they'll sound okay when you add reverb, especially when the rest of the mix is playing.

corrective eq

Changing the EQ of a signal is obviously going to have some effect on the overall sound of that signal, but quite often you'll find your mix includes sounds that occupy only a limited part of the audio spectrum. For example, the overdriven electric guitar contains no really deep bass and the top end rolls off very quickly above 4kHz or so because of the limited response of a guitar speaker. This being the case, you can apply a sharp top cut above 4kHz and a low cut below 100Hz without changing the sound too significantly. You'll have to experiment to find the exactly frequencies, but you'll find this technique very useful, not only with guitars (and bass guitars), but also with warm synth pads from cheap or vintage instruments. Careful use of EQ may also help to reduce the effect of finger noise on stringed instruments.

the wrong sound

Sometimes you find you've made a technically good recording, but the sound just doesn't seem to work in the context of the mix. If EQ doesn't bring results, the tape tracks containing instruments such as electric guitars, bass guitars or organs may be played back through guitar combos and remiked. This way, the speakers will act as filters while the amp EQ also gives you a chance to polish up the basic tone.

The same technique can be used with distorted synth sounds, and just occasionally, you'll find you can hide unwanted distortion by applying even more distortion to the whole track. Admittedly this is more likely to work on an artistic level when used on guitars and synths than it is on, say, vocals or piano!

cases for treatment

While I seldom advocate the use of radical amounts of EQ for acoustic instruments or natural sounds, bass and electric guitars can often benefit from quite assertive equalisation. However, it's little use working on a bass guitar sound in isolation because it will seem totally different when you add the rest of the band. What seems like a wonderfully rich bass sound when soloed can easily dissolve into an indistinct mess when you bring up the rest of the mix. A better way to work is to set up a nominal mix balance, then EQ the bass in context so that it cuts through properly.

Mid-range is very important when creating bass guitar sounds and you may have to apply quite a lot of boost somewhere between 2kHz and 4kHz to get the right edge on the sound. If you boost much higher up, you're into fret noise and string buzz territory, and if you've recorded without a speaker simulator, you might want to roll off some top at the same time.

At the bass end, you can add boost at between 70 and 120Hz to fatten up the sound and a good sweep equaliser or, better still, parametric helps a lot. A simple low shelving EQ will emphasise the bass but may leave you with a poorly defined, muddy bass end. Though most mixing consoles these days have pretty good EQ sections, a quality parametric equaliser is a lot more flexible and every serious studio could use at least one.

guitars

A great electric guitar sound starts out with good playing technique, and the better the player, the simpler the recording technique you can get away with. Interestingly, the most aggressive lead sounds come through turning the distortion amount down, not up. If you use too much overdrive, you end up with a wall of fizz that loses almost the whole of the character of the instrument you're playing. Picking intensity and vibrato are very important as is string bending.

If you've close-miked a guitar amp, you'll still have to add reverb, either using the spring reverb in the amp itself or during the mix using a digital reverb unit. However, try to choose a short, ambient setting rather than a long wash unless the track demands that kind of treatment. You can also experiment with a little slap-back echo to give the sound a clubby, intimate feel. The size of the sound coming off tape has little to do with the physical size or power of your set-up and many classic rock albums have been made using small valve combos.

Chorus, phasing and flanging all work well on guitar, but as a general rule, the more dramatic the effect, the less you need to use it. For example, extreme flanging might work for a couple of bars, whereas gentle chorus can be used all the way through a song.

Guitar players need certain effects to be able to perform properly. Overdrive, wah wah and chorus are examples of commonly used guitar effects, but if you have a spare track, it might pay to make a duplicate DI recording straight from the guitar at the same time. That way, if the sound on your main track doesn't work out, you can take the clean DI'd sound from your extra track and feed it back through an amp or effects unit to create a new guitar sound without having to get the part played again.

vocals

For a natural vocal sound, try to get away with as little EQ as possible, and if you do need EQ, try to get hold of a good quality parametric rather than relying on the EQ in your mixer.

Other than a little compression to keep the level even, and maybe a touch of EQ, all that you need to make your vocal sit properly in the track is reverb. Usually the main vocal will be panned to the centre, with the stereo reverb outputs panned hard left and right to create the illusion of space. Listen carefully to professional records and try to hear the type of reverb they're using; is it long or short, bright or warm? Often you'll find they're using less reverb than you think and many demos sound cluttered simply because there's too much reverb on everything.

In pop music, you're after a hard-hitting sound most of the time, so be sparing in your use of reverb or the impact will be lost. This, incidentally, applies just as much to backing instruments as it does to vocals. Bright reverb sounds are popular on vocals but tend to emphasise any sibilance present in the recording so, again, use your ears and choose a warmer reverb sound if you detect any problems.

stubborn mixes

Occasionally, you'll find a mix that defies all your attempts to balance it satisfactorily, perhaps because the song hasn't been arranged so as to leave space for all the important parts. If you find yourself in this situation, here are a few tricks you can try. Work through the following points and you should end up with something usable.

★ Set up a rough mix, in mono, with no EQ or effects, and see how it sounds.

★   If the mix seems too busy, ask yourself if all the parts are really necessary or can you lose something. What matters most in the majority of pop songs is the rhythm and the vocals, the rest is decoration. If you can't lose something completely, try mixing it so low that you only notice it if you turn it off, or 'squeeze' it using EQ so that it occupies a narrower part of the spectrum. Double checking on headphones can also help you sort out what's clashing with what.

★ If the mid-range sounds are fighting with the bass sounds, again try using EQ to 'thin' out some of them. Take some bottom end out of the pad synth, backing vocals or acoustic guitar parts.

★   Still no luck? Then go back to the basic rhythm section plus vocals and see if that is working. If not, is it too late to try a different drum or bass sound? Similarly, if you're working with a sequencer, you could try picking thinner pad keyboard sounds or brighter bass sounds.

★   Don't overdo effects – reverb creates the illusion of distance and space, yet often you want something to stand out in front. Try using less reverb on upfront sounds to make them 'drier'.

★   If things are improving, try panning the instruments and effects to their desired positions as this will further improve the separation between sounds.

★   Though exciters shouldn't be thought of as a means to salvage poor recordings, the extra separation they create can make the difference between an okay mix and a good one. Use only when you've got everything as good as it can be without it.

★   Perhaps the mix sounds fine but just lacks cohesion or punch. In that case, try a little overall compression. A soft-knee compressor will usually provide the most transparent results, but try whatever you have and let your ears be the judge. Start out with a low ratio of around 2:1 and lower the threshold until you get between 5 and 10dB of gain reduction. Use a 20mS attack time and around a 200mS release time to start with, then adjust by ear making sure you don't squeeze the life out of the track.

the door test

When the mix finally starts to happen, it helps to take a break, have a cup of tea, listen to a few records, and then come back to it. I like to listen to my final mix from the next room with the adjoining door left open, because anything that is too loud or too quiet in the mix is instantly obvious. Strangely, you can miss quite large level discrepancies when you're sitting right in front of the monitors, especially if you're a little tired. Also, play some commercial recordings through your studio system before you mix and listen to these from both inside and outside the room. This should provide an idea of what sort of sound balance you should be aiming at. Some people also like to do a rough mix and check how it sounds on the car stereo or on a ghetto blaster.

Level adjustments are often necessary during the mix, for example, guitars might have to come up slightly during solos and vocal levels may need a little extra 'riding' to keep them under control. However, try to avoid changing the drums or bass levels. If the mix is correctly set up, there probably won't be too much to change, but if things get difficult, get a friend in to help and use a wax pencil to mark where the faders should be at different points in the song. Gates or expanders may be used to clean up tape tracks or the outputs from noisy synths, though care must be taken to ensure the release time of the gate is long enough to prevent slowly decaying sounds from being cut short.

mix compression

It sometimes helps to compress an otherwise finished mix to create the illusion of greater energy, and the best place to patch a compressor is between the multitracker stereo outputs and the input of your stereo tape machine. If you have a separate mixer, then patch the compressor into the mixer's main Left/Right insert points.

Overall compression of this kind causes an overall increase in musical energy which works well on rock, pop and dance material. Some engineers like to add further processing to the stereo mix, including EQ or some kind of harmonic exciter.

using eq

Using EQ could be the subject of a book in its own right, but the real secret is knowing when not to use it. If in doubt, use as little as you can to get the job done, and always use the best outboard EQ you can afford – there's a huge subjective difference between budget models and the high end EQ boxes the pros use.

Equalising the whole mix can improve the sound by helping compensate for limitations in the recording chain, especially true if you're using a cassette multitrack format. A subtle high frequency boost helps create more of a 'digital' sound and you can do this by boosting between 6 and 12kHz using either an external graphic or parametric EQ. Add the EQ sparingly, and if you have access to a parametric model, use a low to medium Q value.

using reverb

Digital reverberation creates the illusion of stereo by synthesising different sets of pseudo random delays for the left and right channels, which makes the reverb patterns slightly different between the left and right outputs. This makes it possible to take a mono tape track and give it both stereo identity and a sense of being somewhere rather than existing in a void. Even if no obvious reverb is needed, a sound can still be given substance and width by adding a very short reverb, ambience or early reflections pattern to it. When you consider that most pop instruments and voices are recorded in mono, the ability of reverberation to simulate a real acoustic space is invaluable in completing the illusion.

For drums and vocals where a longer reverb time is often chosen for artistic reasons, try to pick a setting that doesn't fill up all the space and stifle the mix; it may help to add a pre-delay of around 50mS or so, and if the reverb makes the mix sound muddy, feed it back through a channel with EQ and roll off some of the bottom end. Alternatively, if the reverb is diluting the stereo image of a sound too much, try panning the sound and its reverb to the same point in the mix. This will kill the stereo width effect, but can be effective where a sound needs to come from a precise location.

Avoid putting more than the barest hint of reverb on bass drums or bass instruments unless the mix has loads of empty space to allow the reverb to breathe without clouding the overall picture. Short early reflection or ambience patches seem to work best.

effects with delay

Try panning a signal to one side of the mix with a delayed version (5 – 50mS) panned to the other side. The sound will appear to be coming from the speaker that's carrying the unprocessed sound, even if the delay is as loud as the original signal; although the psychoacoustic reasons why this is so are rather too complex to go into here, it does provide another way to add space to a sound. If the delay is then modulated to produce a chorus sound, the effect is to create the illusion of movement, and when listening in stereo, you really can't tell that one channel is carrying a dry sound and the other a processed version – the movement seems to occupy the whole of the space between the speakers.

Delay can of course be used to create more conventional echo and doubling effects, and it has become fashionable to set up delay times that are multiples of the tempo of the song. For example, if a song is running at 120bpm, each beat is 60 divided by two seconds long – which is half a second. Therefore, a delay of 500mS (half a second), 250mS, or 125mS will always create echoes that are in time with the music. You can also divide the beat time up into threes to create echoes that occur in triplet time.

fades

If a track requires a fade-out ending, make sure you start to fade at least 20 seconds before the recorded material runs out and don't rush the tail end of the fade or it will sound unnatural. If the album is going to be compiled on a hard disk editing system, leave off the fade and do it as part of the editing process; this will be smoother and will fade into true silence.

Once you've recorded your master tape, check it on as many different sound systems as you can to ensure the balance is okay. Listening in the car or on a portable stereo is always a good test.

mastering levels

If you're mastering to cassette, adjust the record level on your mastering cassette recorder so that the loudest signal peaks push the meters around +4dB into the red. I prefer to work without Dolby noise reduction on the mastering recorder but this is largely a matter of personal preference. If you're working with open reel analogue tape, you can probably afford to push the levels a couple of dB further still, but if you're using one of the digital mastering formats, don't allow the peaks to hit the 0VU mark at all. Often the meters on semi-professional DAT and cassette decks won't agree with the meters on the mixer, so for mastering, always go by the meter on the tape machine, not the meters on the desk. It is safest to leave around 30 seconds of unrecorded tape at the beginning of an analogue or DAT cassette to avoid dropouts, and store the finished master in a safe place away from dust, excessive heat, moisture or strong magnetic fields.

Analogue multitrackers, stereo cassette decks and open reel analogue machines should be cleaned before every mixing session as well as before every recording session. Clean the heads and any other metal parts in the tape path with isopropyl alcohol and cotton buds – keep cleaning until the cotton bud comes away clean, then allow the machine to dry for a minute or so before replacing the tape.

coda

Mixing is an acquired skill, so if your first attempts don't come up to scratch, don't let it put you off. You can learn a lot by listening to the production techniques employed on commercial records, and it's also useful to get together with other musicians to swap ideas. Providing you have a clear idea of what you want to achieve, there's no reason why you shouldn't employ the techniques discussed in this book to produce first class demos or even master recordings.

When it comes to choosing equipment, always buy the best you can afford, and as a rule, if it comes to a choice between sound quality and features, put sound quality first. In reality, you can make a good sounding recording with just a basic recorder, a mixer, a reverb unit and a couple of nice mics – the rest can be added when your budget allows. Good luck.

chapter 13

digital recording

The vast majority of modern recording equipment is digital, but to understand its strengths and weaknesses, it's necessary to take a closer look at traditional analogue recording. Analogue tape recording has been with us for many years, but digital recording is still a relatively recent development and is often misunderstood. In some ways, digitising sound is the audio equivalent to cine film, where the constant motion of real life is represented by a series of still frames shown consecutively. As long as there are enough frames per second, the human eye is deceived into perceiving continuous motion. When a sound is digitised, it too is broken up into a series of frozen images, but whereas cinema can be made to work with just 24 frames of film per second, audio needs to be sampled, using an analogue-to-digital converter, at over 40,000 times per second in order to convey full bandwidth audio. Each sample is really just an instantaneous measurement of the voltage of the audio signal as shown in Figure 13.1.

sample rate

Physics dictates that audio must be sampled at a rate at least twice the maximum frequency to be stored, which for 20kHz audio means a sampling rate of at least 40kHz, but in practice, we need to sample at a slightly higher rate to allow for the filters used to exclude audio frequencies above 20kHz. The CD format is based on a sampling rate of 44.1kHz, though some audio applications also sample at 48kHz. Sampling at a lower frequency means limiting the audio bandwidth to less than the 20kHz required by professional audio, but less demanding multimedia applications may sample at 32kHz or less so as to minimise the amount of data needing to be stored.

bits

Sample rate determines the highest frequency we can digitise, but the accuracy of the process also depends on how precisely we can measure each of the tiny slices or samples. As a rule, the more 'bits' used to represent each sample, the less noise and distortion there will be. CDs are sampled with 16-bit resolution, resulting in a possible signal-to-noise ratio of around 96dB –

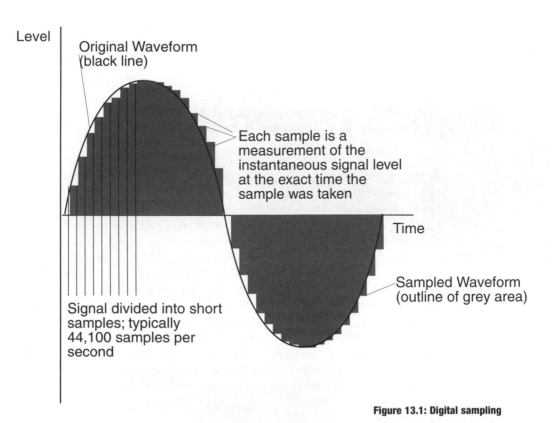

Level

Original Waveform
(black line)

Each sample is a
measurement of the
instantaneous signal level
at the exact time the
sample was taken

Time

Signal divided into short
samples; typically
44,100 samples per
second

Sampled Waveform
(outline of grey area)

Figure 13.1: Digital sampling

significantly better than analogue tape – but once again, for less demanding multimedia applications such as lo-fi computer games, 8-bit sampling may give acceptable results, though the signal-to-noise ratio will be reduced to a rather poor 48dB at best.

Future professional audio formats are likely to require between 18- and 24-bit sampling with the possibility of even higher sample rates, but at the moment, the CD format sets the standard at 44.1kHz sample rate, 16-bits. DAT machines usually offer playback at both 44.1kHz and 48kHz sample rates, though the low cost domestic models that find their way into home studios may only record at the 48kHz sample rate. In theory, a 48kHz sample rate should produce a slightly improved frequency response, but in reality, there is no perceptible difference – at least, not on consumer machines.

evolving digital

Analogue tape recording is unique in that it was developed from the ground up as an audio recording medium, whereas most of the digital formats borrow technology from other market areas, such as the computer, video and hi-fi industries. This makes manufacture commercially viable because of the economies of scale. Analogue recording has been refined over the past few decades to a point where it is unlikely that any further significant improvements will be made, and Dolby SR noise reduction may well be the last hardware breakthrough. By using the latest generation of high energy tapes alongside Dolby SR noise reduction, analogue recorders can provide a dynamic range approaching that of 16-bit digital recorders, and unlike other noise reduction systems, Dolby SR has virtually no audible side effects.

tape saturation

Analogue tape exhibits a magnetic saturation effect when overloaded, which has the result of causing a progressive increase in distortion at higher recording levels. This is rather more friendly than the hard clipping that occurs when digital systems overload, and indeed, analogue tape saturation is used deliberately to create 'warm' sounding recordings. Analogue multitrack obviously still has a lot going for it, and even in this digital age, many people still seek out well-maintained analogue machines specifically for their sound. Ironically, a number of digital processors and software packages are available which set out to process digital data in such a way as to emulate analogue tape saturation effects.

magnetic tape

Any tape recorder suffers from the inherent disadvantage that the tape is in physical contact with the heads and guides of the machine, and this translates into wear, both for the tape itself, and for the metal parts of the recorder. The other obvious disadvantage of a tape-based recording system is that winding the tape from one spool to another takes time.

Accepting the aforementioned limitations, and acknowledging that analogue recorders can sound exceptionally good, the actual results obtained are dependent on the electronic design of the recorder, the mechanics of the transport and the quality of the tape being used. If the tape is not moved across the heads at a perfectly constant speed, then audible effects such as wow and flutter result. Solo piano is a good test for wow and flutter, because it has no natural vibrato. Analogue machines also suffer from modulation noise caused by the way the tape moves over the surface of the head, and though this isn't usually audible when you're recording music, if you try recording a pure sine wave and then play it back, the chances are that it will sound so jittery you'll think the machine is faulty. When you compare this with the same test done on a digital machine, you'll wonder why analogue sounds as good as it does.

sound quality

Given a well set up, properly designed analogue tape machine, the most significant factors affecting sound quality are tape speed and track width. As pointed out in the early chapters of this book, the faster the tape passes over the heads and the wider the tracks (the tape width itself is immaterial), the better the sound quality. An analogue recording is made by magnetising millions of tiny particles of oxide as they pass over the record head, so the recording can be considered as the statistical summation of the magnetic charge of however many of these tiny magnets is passing over the head at any one time. The faster the tape or the wider the tracks, the more particles per second pass over the heads and the more accurate the recording. Photographers will recognise a close analogy between tape noise and film graininess as a function of film speed.

Narrow format open reel machines and cassette multitrack systems don't pass enough oxide over the heads each second to produce an adequately low noise floor so noise reduction systems have to be employed, and all noise reduction systems, to a greater or lesser extent, cause a deterioration in some other aspect of the sound quality. Professionals tend to prefer working with two inch tape running at 30ips without noise reduction. Where noise reduction must be used, Dolby SR is the system of choice for professionals, while for the home user, Dolby S is generally regarded to be the best. Cassette multitrackers are often designed to run at double the normal tape speed so that the noise reduction system chosen doesn't have to work so hard, but even a double speed cassette runs at least four times slower, and has far narrower tracks, than a professional 15ips open reel recorder.

Copying a recording from one tape track to another, as you do when bouncing, causes a loss of quality. Every time an analogue recording is copied, more noise is added and a little more clarity is lost. There can also be problems when playing back tapes recorded on different machines due to small differences in mechanical head alignment, causing a loss of high frequencies.

analogue benefits

Having identified some of the weaknesses of the analogue regime, it's only fair to look at the benefits. Analogue tape recorders have been around for a long time; they work, they're not too difficult to maintain and tape itself is relatively cheap. Tape can spliced, which makes editing easy, and recordings can be kept for many years with minimal deterioration providing they are stored in a suitable environment.

Because you can overdrive analogue tape without getting into hard clipping, you can be a little more casual about recording levels than you have to be with digital systems. When overloaded, digital systems simply clip, and unless the periods of clipping are extremely short, the result is generally audible as a crackle or glitch. It's also possible to varispeed analogue tape over a very large range, you can turn the tape over to create reverse effects, and you can even use two analogue machines to create flanging by using your hand as a brake on one or other of the machine's tape reels. If the worst comes to the worst and you do have a problem with an analogue tape, such as dropout (usually caused by faulty tape or large pieces of foreign material on the heads), you can hear the problem straight away and either redo the recording on a new tape, or try to patch in a piece copied from elsewhere in the song.

Deterioration caused by inappropriate storage is usually gradual and generally involves an overall loss of quality rather than a drastic and complete failure. For all its operational crudities, most audio professionals still seem to feel that analogue tape has the best sound on an artistic level and there's also more confidence in its reliability than there is in digital tape and other digital, tapeless alternatives.

digital tape

There's a lot of rhetoric about the way digital recordings sound, but ultimately, most serious music listening is done via Compact Disk, which is a 16-bit, 44.1kHz digital format with a theoretical maximum dynamic range of 96dB. Even though this is a better dynamic range than you can get from analogue tape used with noise reduction, you have to keep in mind that digital systems have no headroom at all above 0VU – there's no soft clipping as there is with analogue tape. For this reason, when working with digital multitrack, it may be necessary to set the nominal record level at around -12dB on the recorder's own meters, and even then, you still need to keep an eye on the peaks. Once you've allowed a suitable safety margin (headroom), a 16-bit digital system may have little more usable dynamic range than a good analogue recorder working with Dolby SR, so, why is everyone going digital? Perhaps digital systems produce less distortion?

more on sampling

As touched upon in the introduction to this chapter, digital recording systems work by sampling the instantaneous level of the input signal, usually at either 44,100 or 48,000 times a second, then storing these samples as binary numbers. The number of bits defines the precision with which each sample can be taken, and because every sample can only be measured to the nearest whole bit, the digital representation of an analogue waveform is really a series of tiny steps as shown in Figure 13.1. In the case of a 16-bit system, a full-scale signal would occupy 2 to the power of 16 or 65,536 steps, and if the signal being recorded is large, it will use most of the available bits and so be adequately accurate. However, smaller signals will be represented by fewer bits, so the lower the signal level, the higher the percentage of distortion. Analogue tape machines work the other way round – the distortion increases as the level increases.

Another benefit of digital systems is that no noise reduction system is required to achieve in excess of a 90dB signal-to-noise ratio, and, because digital machines are driven from a very accurate, crystal-controlled clock, there's no mechanism by which the recording rate can drift, as there is with analogue where an imperfect capstan shaft or worn pinch roller can compromise the performance. Even with a budget digital system, wow and flutter is effectively eliminated because the digital data goes to and from tape via a crystal-clocked memory buffer.

by the numbers

Once a recording is in the digital domain, it's really just a catalogue of numbers, rather like storing a piece of line art as a precision 'join the dots' drawing. Because we're dealing with absolute numbers, it's possible to copy the data from one digital machine to another or from one track to another simply by duplicating these numbers. The result is a perfect copy with no quality loss.

error correction

In the real world, the numbers occasionally get lost or altered when a transfer takes place, but digital recorders use a very powerful error correction system to enable them to reconstruct small amounts of damaged data, so loss of accuracy is only a problem when something is seriously wrong with either the hardware or the tape. This error correction is vitally important to offset the destructive effects of particles of dirt on the tape's surface and to compensate for minor tape dropouts.

The ability to make a perfectly accurate clone of digital data is of immense value when mastering to DAT or when multitracking on something like the Alesis ADAT or Tascam DA-88, because a second machine will allow you to make safety copies just in case anything should happen to the original.

what can go wrong?

Both analogue and digital tape formats are fine when they're working properly, but what happens when a tape becomes worn or a machine goes out of alignment? With an analogue machine, alignment errors usually lead to a fall-off in the high frequency response of the recording, while a damaged tape may result in momentary dropouts – brief but audible drops in level and/or high end frequency response. Digital machines, on the other hand, deal with absolute numbers, and because some errors are inevitable due to dust on the tape, head wear, tape surface imperfections, their error correction systems are constantly checking for, and repairing corrupted data. A system of recording redundant data enables the machine to verify the data integrity by means of checksums, and small errors can be repaired completely by using the redundant data to reconstruct the original data. This is made possible because the recording process distributes the data on tape in such a way that a brief dropout causes a multitude of small errors over a short period of time rather than causing a large cluster of adjacent errors. If the data were to be recorded linearly, a single dropout would be unrecoverable because all the errors would be in one place.

error concealment

Errors involving a greater amount of data corruption may not leave sufficient information remaining for the error correction to reconstruct the original. It's rather like jabbing a number of small holes in the page of a newspaper; if there are only a few holes, you can work out the missing letters from the context of the undamaged text surrounding the holes, but as the number of holes increases, you'll eventually get to a point where you don't have enough undamaged text to be sure about what's missing. You may still be able to guess, but at some point, even guessing will become impossible.

When this happens to audio data, the system moves from error correction mode to error concealment. In effect, the software looks at the data each side of the problem section and uses interpolation to construct a plausible replacement for the missing data. Technically, this will cause a brief rise in distortion, but usually too brief to be audible. If longer errors occur, then the system can't even make a rough guess as to what's missing so it mutes the audio output until more good data comes along. Only at this point do you notice something is wrong.

While error correction is a wonderful ally, it prevents us from seeing problems develop until it is too late, unless the equipment concerned has some form of error readout system. Sadly, most home studio equipment has little or no error readout facility, and the first you know anything is wrong is when you hear a dropout. Because head wear or recorder misalignment can cause data corruption or misreading problems, it is very important to have digital tape machines serviced on a regular basis, even if no problems are apparent. Most DAT and digital multitrack tape machines should be serviced every 500 hours.

Digital tape can't be edited like analogue tape using razor blades. Editing can be achieved by cloning data from one digital machine to another, but this is time consuming and not everyone has access to two machines. In fact the only really satisfactory way to edit digital material is to use a hard disk editing system, and these are described later in the chapter.

For routine work where little or no editing is needed, analogue tape is probably still the easiest medium to use and it has fewer complications. Digital tape recording is a seductive concept, but inexperienced users might find that their recordings are just as noisy as they ever were because the major source of noise isn't usually the recording system – it's the material being fed into it. However, digital tape has the benefit that recordings can be cloned, there's no wow and flutter, and the media cost is low.

dcc

Before leaving digital tape recording systems, it is appropriate to mention the Philips DCC (Digital Compact Cassette) format. This is a consumer system that uses data reduction algorithms to simplify the audio signal to the extent that it can be recorded onto tape by means of a stationary, multichannel head. The result is technically inferior to DAT and CD insomuch as data reduction can be shown to have audible side effects on some types of material, but to put it in perspective, the side effects are less serious than from most types of semi-pro (and indeed most professional) analogue tape noise reduction systems. The vast majority of people are unable to differentiate between DCC and CD on commercial pop music, but classical music may show up a lack of detail or a reduction in the sense of space.

At the time of writing, DCC machines are being sold very cheaply, which makes them a viable, and far superior option to analogue cassette in a home studio environment. Portable versions are also available for location sound gathering and for recording samples. The digital data from a DCC machine can be transferred to DAT but DCC can't be used for backing up digital data from hard disk recorders because of the data reduction algorithms used. As a home recording mastering format, DCC is fine, but there are doubts over the future of the format, so if DCC machines are still available by the time you read this and you're thinking of buying one, it's probably a good idea to buy in a stock of blank tapes at the same time.

hard disk recording

Even as recently as the early nineties, tapeless recording was too expensive for most home recording enthusiasts to contemplate, but now the cost of the hardware has plummeted to the point that it's probably the cheapest way to get into multitrack recording – and it looks set to continue getting cheaper. Using a computer, such as an AV Macintosh or a Pentium PC fitted with a suitable soundcard and a large capacity hard drive, you can experiment with tapeless recording and editing for very little more than the cost of a suitable computer and some software.

Alternatively, there are stand-alone, hard disk-based digital workstations, the first truly low cost models being the Fostex DMT-8 and the Roland VS-880. The reason prices have fallen so significantly is that unlike analogue recording, the hardware used in tapeless systems is based on the same components as used elsewhere in the computer industry, and the demands of multimedia keep on pushing the price down and the performance up.

tapeless quality

16-bit hard disk recording can provide the same audio quality as CD, and indeed, the quality should be better than digital tape, because unlike tape, hard disk error correction systems always reconstruct the original data – guesswork isn't in their nature! However, audio fidelity is also dictated by the quality of the analogue-to-digital and digital-to-analogue converters used in the product. For example, high quality converters in an external rack box are likely to sound every bit as good as CD, while budget converters residing in a computer, either as part of the basic hardware or a soundcard, are much more likely to pick up noise from the computer's own electronics. They may also use low cost converter chips which offer relatively poor resolution resulting in increased noise and distortion. As with other aspects of digital systems, converters are improving at an impressive rate.

hard drives

Tapeless multitrack recorders usually store their data onto computer hard drives or onto some form of removable disk. Currently, not all hard disk drives are suitable for recording multitrack audio, though most new computers come equipped with so-called AV drives, which can usually handle up to at least eight tracks of simultaneous playback. Standard computer drives take short breaks to recalibrate themselves to offset the effects of temperature changes, and while the buffer memory may be large enough to ensure this doesn't interrupt the data flow, if you're recording or playing back more than a couple of tracks, you may hear breaks in the audio.

The more tracks you intend to play back at one time, the more serious the problem becomes, which is why the so-called AV drives were developed. These have intelligent thermal recalibration systems that avoid interrupting when the disk is reading or writing data, making them a better choice for multitrack work.

random access

Computer hard drives can move to any piece of data within a few milliseconds, which is a great benefit for audio users. Random access means you don't have to wait for tape to wind to get where you want to go, but the advantages of random access go much further than simply avoiding tape rewinding time. By using random access memory as a buffer, audio can be read onto and off a disk in a continuous, uninterrupted stream, which opens up all kinds of interesting editing possibilities. For example, you can access any section of recorded audio data in any order, rearrange the sections into a new order, then play back your new arrangement.

destructive editing

Being able to rearrange, copy or remove material without altering the original data file is known as non-destructive editing, and there's a lot you can do to a recording without changing the original data in any way. Nevertheless, there are times when you may want a change to become permanent – for example, when silencing the noise immediately prior to the start of a song or changing the actual level of the recorded audio. On a computer-based system, you may even be able to zoom in on a tiny section of the audio waveform to wipe out an annoying guitar squeak or similar noise.

The main editing tricks you can do with digital systems are based around rearranging your material in a different order, but you can also normalise signal levels to bring the peaks up to 0dB, apply digital EQ, reverse sections of sound, create fade-ins and outs, and a number of other things that would have been difficult or impossible using tape. More sophisticated systems allow you to use plug-in, software-based effects (the software equivalents of separate signal processors or effects units), such as reverb, delay, compression, stereo enhancement, de-noising, click removal, 3D spacial enhancement and so forth.

media costs

Currently, disks are considerably more expensive than tape – though it's surely only a matter of time before suitable high capacity drives fall to around the same price (based on recording time) as tape. One minute of mono audio requires around 5Mbytes of drive space, though this can be reduced by up to a factor of four if a data-compressed audio format is used. It isn't practical to archive to fixed disk drives in the same way as it is tape – but it's possible to use a tape-based data backup system such as Exobyte, or data DAT, which at the time of writing is still considerably cheaper than removable disk media. Backing up to and reloading from digital tape is obviously very slow, but the cost saving may make it worthwhile for the home user where time isn't so pressing as it is in the commercial environment.

audio with midi

The ability to record audio directly onto the hard drive of an ordinary computer gets really exciting when you combine it with MIDI. Virtually all leading sequencer manufacturers now produce software packages that integrate the recording and editing of MIDI data with the recording and editing of audio. In other words, any audio you record can be accessed and arranged in much the same way as you arrange your sequenced MIDI patterns, from the same sequencer arrange page. Everything is done from the same computer, and you don't have to keep changing your mental outlook as you switch from working with MIDI data to audio data.

If you work with MIDI already, then adding a few tracks of direct-to-disk audio is a very practical and flexible way to put a complete recording studio on your desktop. Little additional hardware is needed – the audio is automatically synchronised to the MIDI data – and even 'virtual' effects can be added inside the computer providing you have the right software and a reasonably powerful computer. Even a more sophisticated system is only likely to need the addition of a small mixer, a few synth modules and one or two effects boxes. Furthermore, because a typical MIDI composition may only include a small amount of audio, removable media drives become more cost effective as a storage medium.

hard disk editors

Hard disk editors exist specifically to manipulate and rearrange stereo material, their most common applications involving compiling individual tracks to produce a Production Master tape for an album project or to rearrange the sections of a song to create a new version. Such editing systems are often used to create extended remixes or to shorten songs. Sophisticated crossfading algorithms are used to ensure that there are no audible glitches at the edit points – something that isn't always true when editing analogue tape using razor blades. Tapeless editing may also be used to assemble the best parts of several different versions of the same piece of music or dialogue.

While basic cut and paste editing is possible on a multitrack hard disk system, a dedicated stereo editing system or software package will usually include specialist tools that can be used to edit audio to a much finer degree, though the features of both multitrack systems and editors are now staring to converge. Other software tools include utilities for PQ coding CD masters (adding the pause and cue information), and for burning writable CDs to produce one-off CD masters from your DAT original.

practicalities

With any computer-based audio recording system, it is advisable to use a separate drive to store your audio. Audio drives need to be emptied or defragmented pretty regularly, and if you have all your other software and system files residing on the same drive, this becomes more difficult. With a separate drive, all you need do is back up finished projects, then erase all the data on the drive ready for the next session.

Stereo material sampled at 44.1kHz uses around 10Mbytes of disk space per minute, which means approximately 600Mbytes of disk space is required to record an hour's worth of stereo material. In reality, you need rather more, because if you decide to do a destructive edit, the system usually creates backup files so that you can undo any changes that don't work out as planned. For this reason, a 1Gbyte drive should be considered the bare minimum for a typical album project, though with drive prices as low as they are, a 2Gbyte or 4Gbyte drive is a better bet. As a rule, larger capacity drives are also faster, which means you can record and play back more tracks simultaneously in a multitrack system.

With multitracking, available disk space is shared out between however many tracks you want to record, so it follows that the recording time is halved every time you double the number of tracks. Using a 600Mbyte drive, you can expect a maximum of a quarter of an hour of continuous 8-track or less than eight minutes of 16-track recording time.

input/output options

How audio gets in and out of your system depends on the hardware you have. Low end soundcards often have analogue inputs and outputs only, while more sophisticated cards may include S/PDIF and/or AES/EBU digital interfaces. Providing the analogue inputs are of reasonable quality, they'll probably be fine for multitrack work – after all, most of the source material is analogue. However, for editing stereo material, it's generally considered unacceptable to leave the digital domain unless you specifically need to treat the audio using an analogue processor of some kind.

Audio data to be edited is generally fed in from DAT via the digital I/O connectors, but it's advisable to buy a proper digital transfer cable. While you may get away using a hi-fi phono lead, you could equally end up with inexplicable clicks and glitches!

integrated tapeless workstations

Hard disk recording systems require DSP power to process audio data, and the more processing you need to do at one time, the more processing power is required. Some card-based systems allow you to add more DSP power in the form of additional cards, either fitted inside the computer or in an expansion chassis. Nevertheless, such systems are currently expensive and are more likely to appeal to professionals able to make a commercial return on their investment.

The other option is to choose a hardware-based audio workstation combining tapeless recording, mixing and effects. These tend to have fewer features than their computer-based cousins, but they are invariably more straightforward to use, and the usual minefield of computer problems and conflicts is neatly avoided. More importantly, if it stops working, you know where the blame lies, whereas if a computer system packs in, the software manufacturer will probably blame the hardware and vice versa!

Currently, cassette-based multitrackers are being superseded by Data MiniDisc-based 4-track machines, and though four tacks may not seem like much to play with, with a MIDI sequencer locked to such a machine via MIDI Time Code (MTC), there's a lot of creative potential. What's more, Data MiniDiscs are more cost effective to archive than any other form of removable media presently available. MiniDisc uses an aggressive data compression system to maximise the recording time available from a disk, but in reality, the side-effects of data compression are far less serious than those of the analogue tape noise reduction systems that went before. While uncompressed audio remains the preferred choice for professional applications, formats like MiniDisc provide an affordable, good sounding alternative for the private studio owner or recording musician.

future imperfect?

In the future, we'll probably see more computer-based, direct-to-disk systems connected to dedicated hardware control surfaces so that they combine the advantages of the digital environment with the controls surface of a conventional analogue-style mixer. Such interfaces are currently available, but are expensive. However, as computers become more powerful, the need for hardware control will become greater and market pressure should result in lower cost user interfaces.

Once again, the multimedia market will probably be largely responsible for the next generation of products, and within a very short space of time it'll be possible to perform even more sophisticated multitrack recording and editing using nothing more than an off-the-shelf multimedia PC and a suitable software package. However, media compatibility is likely to become a major issue as new drive formats appear monthly, few of which are compatible with their predecessors. There will also be serious clock synchronisation issues to be addressed once fully digital recording systems, comprising multiple separate pieces of equipment, become commonplace in the private studio.

In the longer term, we can expect solid-state rather than disk storage, but in the shorter term, I believe that analogue tape, digital tape and disk-based recording will continue to coexist amicably for a number of years yet.

glossary of terms

Audio:

> The area of technology related to sound recording, processing, amplification and reproduction.

AC:

> Alternating Current – a dynamic electrical signal that regularly changes from positive to negative polarity. Audio signals are an example of alternating current, though the term more normally applies to mains electricity power supplies operating at a fixed frequency.

AES/EBU:

> Digital interfacing standard for transferring stereo audio data from one system to another. The connection standard is a balanced XLR and regular mic cables may be used for short distance communication, though specialised digital cable is recommended.

Active:

> Circuit containing components that can amplify such as valves, ICs, transistors or FETs. Circuits that work purely by resistive, capacitive, inductive or diodic action are classified as passive.

A to D converter:

> Device for converting analogue signals to a stream of digital numbers. The signal is sampled at frequency regular intervals and the instantaneous level represented as a binary number.

ADT:

> Automatic Double Tracking. A term used to describe the use of a short echo to simulate the effect of the same sound being recorded twice. See Double Tracking.

Ambience:

> The perceived effect of the environment on a sound heard within that environment due to sound reflections and absorption from surfaces. Heavily reflective environments are said to be reverberant.

Amp:

> Abbreviation for Ampere, the standard unit of electrical current. Fuses are rated in Amps. A current of one thousandth of an Amp is one milliamp or 1mA.

Amplify:

> To increase the amplitude (magnitude) of an electrical signal.

Amplitude:

> The level or magnitude of an electrical signal expressed in Volts.

Analogue:

> A continuously varying electrical signal (unlike digital signals which comprise a series of steps).

Anechoic:

> Acoustic environment designed to absorb virtually all sound so as to produce no significant reflections.

Attenuate:

    To reduce the level of an electrical signal.

Aux Send:

    A mix buss output designed specifically for driving external effects or foldback systems. See pre-fade and post-fade.

Axis:

    Imaginary line depicting the primary direction of transmission or reception of an audio transducer.

Backup:

    Safety copy of tape or software.

Balance:

    Ratio of the left and right channels in a stereo system.

Balancing:

    Cabling system using two out-of-phase conductors within a common screen. When balanced equipment is connected onto both ends of the cable, any interference affecting the cable is cancelled out resulting in a cleaner signal. Most microphones used in recording are balanced.

Band:

    A specific range of frequencies. In audio, this usually means a section of the audio spectrum.

Bandwidth:

    The range of frequencies passed by an electronic circuit.

Boost/Cut Control:

    Control which allows a range of frequencies to be either increased or decreased in level. In the centre position, the control has no effect.

Bias Signal:

    A high frequency signal which is recorded onto analogue tape along with the audio signal. This signal is inaudible but is necessary for accurate recording.

Binary:

    Numbering system comprising 1s and 0s. Binary mathematics is the basis of virtually all computers.

Bit:

    Term describing the smallest piece of binary information, which may be either a 1 or a 0.

Bounce:

    The process of mixing two or more tracks from a multitrack recorder and simultaneously recording the result back to another track.

Buffer:

    Section of computer RAM memory used for temporary storage of information. Term may also be used to describe an analogue circuit designed to isolate the effects of one circuit from another circuit connected to it. For example, a buffer circuit on the output of one device may be used to prevent the next piece of equipment in line from loading the output of the first device.

Buss:

    An electrical signal path onto which other signals may be mixed. In a mixer or multitracker, different busses are provided to carry the stereo mix, the signals being mixed to tape, the aux sends and so on. The term buss is also used for power cables that supply numerous destinations, for example, to the individual circuit boards inside a mixer.

Byte:

A piece of digital data comprising eight bits.

C-60:

Cassette tape designed to provide a total of 60 minutes' playing time when used in a conventional cassette deck. When used in a multitracker, the maximum playing time will be reduced to 30 minutes because the tape is played only in one direction (it is not turned over when it reaches the end). In some multitrackers, the tape speed is double that of a hi-fi machine in order to provide higher sound quality. This halves the maximum playing time again meaning that a C-60 tape will provide a maximum of 15 minutes' recording.

Cable:

Insulated electrical conductor, for example, a power cord or signal lead.

Cannon Connector:

Proprietary brand of XLR connector.

Capacitor:

Electronic component comprising two spaced conductors coupled electrostatically. The space between the conductors may be air or some other non-conducting dielectric.

Capacitor Microphone:

A professional recording microphone that works by small changes in electrical capacitance. Capacitor microphones require phantom power to operate, usually 48V.

Cardioid:

A type of microphone pickup pattern relating to a mic that picks up sounds from mainly one direction. These mics may also be known as unidirectional.

Channel:

A mixer or multitracker signal input path and its associated controls. MIDI systems also operate on one of 16 channels – see chapter on MIDI.

Chase:

The process whereby the slave device in a master/slave synchronisation system attempts to achieve sync with the master.

Chorus:

Effect using delay and pitch modulation to create the effect of two or more musicians playing the same part.

Clipping:

Type of distortion where the top of a waveform is truncated above a certain threshold. Usually occurs when a circuit is forced to handle a signal level higher than it was designed to.

Clock:

Electronic circuit designed to generate precisely spaced pulses for timing applications, such as analogue to digital conversion or to drive a digital processor.

Clone:

> Exact copy. In digital recording, the term relates to a digital transfer of a tape or disk where the data is exactly identical to that of the original.

Compander:

> Circuit with both compressor and expander stages, usually for use in a noise reduction system.

Compressor:

> Processor for reducing the dynamic range of an audio signal.

Conductor:

> A material that presents little resistance to the flow of electrical current.

Continuous Controller:

> A control that provides smoothly variable control rather than obviously switched steps. Of course, in digital circuits, and in MIDI, all changes are made up of discrete steps, but providing the changes between successive steps are small enough, the result is perceived as being continuous.

Control Voltage:

> A varying voltage used to control one or more parameters of a circuit.

CrO2:

> Type of recording tape based on a Chromium oxide compound. Also known as Type II. Most multitrackers are designed to give the best results with Type II tapes.

Cut-Off Frequency:

> The frequencies at which the gain of an amplifier or filter falls by 3dB.

Cut and Paste.

> An editing term that originated with word processing to describe the process of copying or moving data from one place to another.

D to A Converter:

> Circuit for converting a digitised signal back into an analogue signal. Also known as a DAC.

Daisy Chain:

> To connect two or more devices in series (the output of one device feeds the input of the next device along, and so on).

Damping:

> The control exercised by the output stage of an amplifier on a loudspeaker's attempt to overshoot. Damping factor is calculated as the load (speaker) impedance divided by the output impedance of the amplifier.

DAT:

> Digital Audio Tape used with DAT recorders.

Data:

> Information stored in a digital (usually binary) form.

dB:

> Short for deciBel. Used to express the relative levels of two electrical voltages, powers or sounds.

dBm:
> Reference level where 0dBm = 1mW into 600 Ohms.

dBv:
> Reference level where 0dBv = 0.775 Volts.

dBu:
> Same as dBv.

dBV:
> Reference level where 0dBv = 1 Volt.

dB per octave:
> A measure of the slope of a filter circuit.

dbx:
> Type of tape noise reduction system.

DC:
> Direct current.

Decay:
> The time taken for a reverberatory or echoing sound to fall in level by 60dB. Also used to describe the closing of an envelope generating circuit.

Desk:
> Alternative word for mixer or console.

Depth:
> The amount by which one parameter is modulated by another, for example, vibrato or chorus depth.

Detent:
> Mechanical 'click' designed to indicate the centre of the travel of a rotary control such as a pan pot of EQ cut/boost control.

Dielectric:
> The insulating layer between the two conductors of a capacitor.

Digital Audio:
> Electronic device that works by representing electrical signals as a series of binary numbers.

Digital Delay:
> Digital processor for generating delay or echo effects.

Digital Reverb:
> Digital processor for recreating reverberation.

DIN Connector:
> Type of multipin connector with several possible pin configurations. MIDI uses a 5-pin, 180 degree DIN plug and socket.

Disc:

> Media in the form of a disc, such as CD or MiniDisc. Excludes computer floppy and hard disks, which end with the letter k to signify that they are abbreviations of the word diskette.

Disk Drive:

> Mechanism for reading and writing computer floppy or hard disks. Fixed hard drives include a disk that cannot be removed.

Display:

> Computer monitor or some form of alphanumeric readout built from LCDs or LEDs.

Distortion:

> Any measurable difference, other than in amplitude, between an input signal and an output signal.

Dither:

> System of adding a low level noise to digital signals so as to produce smoother low signal performance at the expense of slightly increased background noise.

Dolby:

> Type of tape noise reduction system. Dolby B, C and S are used in both hi-fi and semi-pro recording equipment while Dolby SR and Dolby A are only used in professional applications.

Double Tracking:

> The process of recording the same performance twice, onto two different tape tracks. When the two parts are played back, the effect of two people playing or singing together is created. Double tracking is often employed to thicken up the sound of a weak vocalist.

Driver:

> Term used to describe the mechanical part of a loudspeaker. Also used to describe a piece of software that enables a hardware peripheral or internal card to interface with a computer.

Dry Signal:

> A sound source which has no added effect. Conversely, a sound treated with an effect such as reverberation or echo is often referred to as wet.

Ducking:

> The process of controlling the level of one audio signal by another.

Dynamic Microphone:

> Microphone that uses a moving coil in a magnetic field to generate an output signal

Dynamic Range:

> The range between the highest and lowest levels of a signal. Usually expressed in dBs.

Edit:

> To change recorded data, or computer stored digital data, in some way.

Echo:

> Effect created by repeating the original signal, often several times, after a short time delay.

Effect:

> A device designed to add special effects to a sound. Examples are: delay, reverb, pitch shifting, chorus, flanging, ADT, phasing and vibrato.

Effects Send:
> Mixer output designed to feed an external effects unit.

Effects Return:
> Additional mixer input used to feed an effects unit back into the mix.

Electret Microphone:
> Type of microphone based on a permanently charged capacitor capsule.

Envelope:
> The overall amplitude contour of an electrical waveform.

Erase:
> To remove data from a recording system and replace it by silence. Recordings may also be erased by recording new material in place of the original material.

Equaliser:
> Device used to selectively increase or decrease the level of specific parts of the audio spectrum relative to others.

Expander:
> Audio processor designed to increase the dynamic range of a signal. Conceptually like a compressor in reverse.

Expander Module:
> Usually describes a MIDI sound module, though may also be used to describe an add-on to provide a mixer with more channels.

Fader:
> Slider control, as opposed to rotary control.

Ferric:
> Type of recording tape composition. Ferric tapes are usually the cheapest but don't produce as high a quality result as CrO2 or Type II tapes.

Filter:
> A circuit that amplifies or attenuates a specific band of frequencies.

Flanging:
> Delay effect using modulation and feedback to produce a sweeping sound.

Foldback:
> Also known as Cue. System for providing performers with a separate mix which they can listen to while recording or overdubbing.

Format:
> Process done to a computer disk before it can be used to store data. Formatting effectively creates 'compartments' into which data can be stored.

Frequency:
> Number of cycles of a repetitive waveform that occur each second.

Frequency Response:
> A measurement of the frequency range that can be accurately handled by a piece of electrical equipment, microphone or loudspeaker.

FSK:
> Frequency Shift Keying. A system for representing MIDI Clock pulses as bursts of audio tones that can be recorded onto tape.

FX:
> Slang term for 'effects'.

Gain:
> The amount by which a signal is amplified.

Gate:
> Device for shutting off a signal when it falls below a specific threshold level.

Glitch:
> Unwanted pop or click that gets recorded to tape, often due to electrical interference from an outside source.

Graphic Equaliser:
> An equaliser using several faders, each to provide cut or boost over a narrow range of frequencies.

Ground:
> Electrical connection to earth.

Ground Loop:
> Wiring problem that causes unwanted hum to be added to an audio signal.

Hard Disk Recording:
> The process of recording digitised audio onto a hard disk rather than onto tape.

Harmonic:
> High frequency component of a waveform at a multiple of the fundamental frequency.

Harmonic Distortion:
> The addition of harmonics not originally present in a signal.

HF:
> High Frequency.

High Pass Filter:
> Filter that passes signals above a specified frequency and attenuates those falling below that frequency.

Inductor:
> Electrical component, usually some form of coil, that exhibits inductance. Inductors have a higher impedance at high frequencies than they have at low frequencies.

Insulator:
> Material with very high resistance that effectively prevents an electrical current from flowing.

Impedance:
>The 'AC resistance' of a circuit.

Interface:
>A device that converts one form of data or signal to another. For example, a MIDI interface allows MIDI information to be generated and read by a computer.

Insert Point:
>Connection socket allowing an external processor to be 'inserted' in series with a signal.

I/O:
>Input/Output.

ips:
>Inches per second.

Jack Plug:
>Common semi-pro recording and instrument audio connector. May be either mono or stereo.

Jack Socket:
>Receptacle for jack plug.

Keyboard:
>Musical interface based on the piano keyboard but electrical in operation. Also applies to computer keyboard, which is based on the QWERTY typewriter.

kHz:
>Multiples of 1000Hz or 1000 cycles of a waveform per second.

kOhm:
>1000 Ohms.

LCD:
>Liquid Crystal Display.

LED:
>Light Emitting Diode. Type of solid-state lamp.

LFO:
>Low Frequency Oscillator used as a control source rather than a sound source.

Limiter:
>Device which prevents an audio signal from exceeding a set level. Signals below this level are unaffected.

Logic:
>Type of circuitry used to process digital signals.

Loop:
>Circuit where the output has a path back to the input.

Low Pass Filter:
>Circuit that passes signals below a set frequency and attenuates those above it.

mA:
> Milliamp; one thousandth of an amp.

M (pronounced Meg):
> Abbreviation for 1,000,000. Examples are MHz, M Ohm and so on.

Memory:
> Circuit used to store digital data.

Metal:
> Type of tape formulation capable of producing very high quality recordings. Metal tape can only be used in machines specifically designed to take metal tape.

Microprocessor:
> Chip at the heart of desktop computers and other digital devices.

Modulate:
> To vary some aspect of a signal (or digital representation of a signal), by means of another signal or waveform.

Monitor:
> In recording terms, Monitor means to listen over loudspeakers or headphones.

Mono:
> Single channel of audio information for reproduction over a single speaker. If multiple speakers are used, they all carry exactly the same signal.

Multitrack:
> The process of recording a piece of music using a multitrack recording device so that different parts may be recorded at different times.

Multitracker:
> A single piece of equipment which combines a multitrack tape recorder with a mixer. When spelled with a capital M, the term is a registered trademark of Fostex. The term Portastudio is also used generically by some people, but this is actually a trademark of the TEAC corporation. To my knowledge, there is no widely used generic term for a cassette multitracker that doesn't rely on one or other of these brand names.

Multitimbral:
> A synthesizer or module capable of playing back two or more sounds simultaneously, each controlled by a separate MIDI channel. The majority of modern multitimbral instruments can produce either eight or 16 simultaneous parts.

Noise Gate:
> See Gate.

(Tape) Noise Reduction:
> Systems such as Dolby or dbx are specific examples of encode/decode noise reduction systems insomuch as they process the signal during recording and then apply the opposite process on playback. The processing is designed to bring about a decrease in tape hiss, though it doesn't affect any hiss that may have been recorded as part of the original signal.

Normalise:

A socket wired so that the original signal path is unaffected unless a plug is inserted into the socket. Mixer insert points are normalised as are some types of patchbay connection.

Octave:

A range of frequencies where the upper limit is twice the lower frequency.

Off Line:

Non-real-time process.

Ohm:

Unit of electrical resistance. 1,000 Ohms is expressed as 1K Ohm and 1,000,000 Ohms is expressed as 1M Ohm.

Ohm's Law:

Formula relating resistance, voltage and current in a resistive circuit. $I=V/R$ where I is the current in Amps, V is the voltage and R is resistance in Ohms.

Open Circuit:

A break in a circuit preventing current flow.

Operating System:

The basic 'housekeeping' software used by a computer to allow it to run other software, communicate with peripherals and run a display.

Oscillator:

Electronic circuit that produces a repeating waveform.

Overdub:

To record onto a new track of a multitrack recorder while monitoring what has already been recorded on the other tracks.

Overload:

To exceed the limits for which a circuit has been designed.

Pad:

Resistive circuit designed to reduce the level of a signal.

Pan Control:

Control for moving a signal between the left and right stereo extremes.

Parallel:

To connect two or more electrical components or systems so that all their inputs are connected together, and all their outputs are connected together.

Passive:

An electrical circuit that contains no active (amplifying) components. For example, a resistive pad is a passive circuit.

Parametric EQ:

A band-pass equaliser providing independent control over cut/boost, frequency and bandwidth.

Patchbay:
> Panel-mounted connectors used to bring commonly used inputs and outputs to a central location. Signal routing is changed using plug-in patch cords.

Patch Cord:
> Short cable for use with patch bays.

Phantom Power:
> A system for supplying 48V power to balanced capacitor and electret microphones via a standard microphone cable. The phantom power source may be a stand-alone unit, but is more often built into the mixing console or the mic preamp being used.

Phase:
> The timing difference between two electrical waveforms expressed in degrees. 360 degrees represents a delay of one complete cycle.

Phase Shift:
> The change of phase in a signal relative to its original form via time delay or other electrical/electronic processing.

Phaser:
> Modulated delay effect which mixes a signal with a phase shifted version of itself to produce a filtering effect.

Phasing:
> Studio effect created by adding a phase shifted signal to a non-phase shifted signal, then varying the amount of phase shift.

Phono Plug:
> Type of signal connector used on hi-fi and semi-pro recording equipment.

Pitch:
> Frequency or musical note.

Power Supply:
> Converts mains electricity to the voltages required to power a piece of electronic equipment.

Post-Fade:
> Aux signal derived from after a mixer's channel fader so that the aux send level reflects any channel fader adjustments. Post-fade sends are generally used for feeding effects devices and may be referred to as effects sends.

Pre-Fade:
> Aux signal derived from before the channel fader so that the aux send level is independent of the channel fader position. Pre-fade sends are often used for creating Foldback or Cue mixes and may be referred to as Foldback controls.

Program Change:
> MIDI command for changing synthesizer or effect programs.

Punch In:
> Also known as 'dropping in'. Describes the action of putting a tape track into record while the tape is in motion so as to replace a specific section of a recording.

Punch Out:
> The action terminating a punch-in by switching the tape machine out of record.

PZM:
> Pressure Zone Microphone, also known as Boundary Microphone.

Q:
> Measure of resonance of a filter circuit, defined as centre frequency divided by bandwidth.

Quantise:
> The division of information into equally spaced time divisions. For example, quantising MIDI data will place each note to the nearest 1/16 of a bar (or whatever quantisation resolution is selected).

RAM:
> Random Access Memory.

R-DAT:
> Rotary Head, Digital Tape Machine.

Real Time:
> Process that takes place with no perceptible delay.

Resistance:
> Opposition to the flow of electrical current, measured in Ohms.

Resonance:
> The degree to which a filter circuit or mechanical resonator emphasises a particular frequency. See Q.

Reverberation:
> Natural effect created when a sound bounces off nearby solid surfaces in an enclosed space.

S/PDIF:
> A digital standard interfacing system for transferring stereo audio data from one piece of equipment to another. The connection format is RCA phono connector, but specialised digital cable should be used.

Sample:
> The process of digitising a signal by measuring successive points along an analogue waveform. A sampler is also a type of synthesizer that uses recorded sounds as its source. These recorded sounds are also called samplers.

Separation:
> Keeping sounds separate. In a studio where several musicians are playing together, each player's mic will tend to pick up some sound from the other instruments in the room. The lower the level of this unwanted spill, the better the separation.

Sequencer (MIDI):
> Device for the recording, editing and replay of MIDI music compositions. May be computer-based or a piece of stand-alone hardware.

Single-ended:
> A process that may be used in one stage, unlike double-ended systems requiring encoding at

one stage and decoding at another.

Signal:

Any meaningful electrical information passing through an electronic system.

Signal-To-Noise Ratio:

The ratio of the maximum signal level to the circuit or tape noise in dBs.

Short Circuit:

Term used to describe an accidental signal path between two points in a circuit not normally connected.

SMPTE:

Time code used in film soundtrack work, music and recording.

Spill:

Term used to describe unwanted sound leakage into microphones. For example, in a live situation, the drums and guitar amps will invariably spill into the vocal mics.

SPL:

Sound Pressure Level.

Stereo:

Two-channel system feeding left and right loudspeakers in an attempt to recreate the way we perceive sounds coming from different directions.

Sync:

Synchronisation – a process for making two or more time-dependent devices start together and run at exactly the same speed.

Synthesizer:

Musical instrument able to generate a wide variety of musically pitched sounds by electronic means.

Thru:

See MIDI Thru.

Track:

Originally a tape-based term, track relates to the physical section of tape used to store individual parts of the recording. Tracks are parallel to each other and are recorded and played back using a multisection head so as to keep them separate until they are mixed. The term has now been carried over to digital tape and hard disk recording systems, though it is mainly conceptual in this context insomuch as the data is not recorded on individual, parallel tracks.

Transpose:

To change the musical key or pitch of a note or sequence of notes.

Unbalanced:

Conventional audio connection with a single signal conductor surrounded by a screen.

Unison:

Musical term relating to two or more instruments, or sounds, playing the same notes at the same time.

Valve:

Active circuit device involving a heated cathode, a grid and an anode sealed in an evacuated glass tube. Also known as tubes.

VCA:

Voltage Controlled Amplifier.

VCF:

Voltage Controlled Filter.

VCO:

Voltage Controlled Oscillator.

Velocity:

Measure of how hard a note is played on a MIDI keyboard.

Vibrato:

Musical, low frequency modulation of pitch.

Volt:

Unit of measurement of electrical potential energy.

Watt:

Unit of electrical power.

Wah:

Filter sweep effect, originally developed for use in guitar pedals.

Waveform:

Visual representation of an electrical signal.

White Noise:

Random electrical signal with equal average energy per Hz.

XLR:

Type of pro-audio connector commonly used to carry balanced audio signals including microphones.

Zero Crossing:

The point at which an AC waveform switches from positive to negative voltage, and vice versa.

basic midi jargon

MIDI:

Musical Instrument Digital Interface.

Note On:

MIDI message sent when note is played (key pressed).

Note Off MIDI:

Message sent when key is released.

MIDI Module:

Sound generating device with no integral keyboard.

Multitimbral Module:

> MIDI Sound Source capable of producing several different sounds at the same time and controlled on different MIDI channels.

MIDI Channel:

> The 16 channels over which MIDI information can be sent.

MIDI Mode:

> MIDI information can be interpreted by the receiving MIDI instrument in a number of ways, the most common being polyphonically on a single MIDI channel (Poly-Omni Off mode). Omni mode enables a MIDI instrument to play all incoming data regardless of channel.

MTC:

> MIDI Time Code; a MIDI equivalent of SMPTE time code using the same time and frame parameters as SMPTE. Unlike SMPTE, MTC is incorporated into the MIDI data stream and can be passed down the same MIDI cable as other MIDI data.

MIDI Program Change:

> Type of MIDI message used to change sound patches on a remote module or the effects patch on a MIDI effects unit.

MIDI Controller:

> MIDI message sent in response to movement of certain physical controls on the Master keyboard (or other MIDI instrument).

MIDI Merge:

> Device for combining two streams of MIDI data.

MIDI Sync:

> A system of synchronising two or more pieces of compatible equipment using MIDI Clock, a tempo-related timing signal of 96 pulses per quarter note.

mixer jargon

those numbers!

> If you see a mixer described as a 24:8:24:2, the first number is the number of input channels. The second number, in this case 8, means the mixer has eight output groups. The third number tells us how many monitor channels the desk has, and if it's an in-line desk, this will be the same as the number of input channels. If, on the other hand it is a split console, the number of monitor channels may well be less than the number of input channels. Finally, the number 2 indicates that the main output of the desk is stereo.

In-Line:

> Means the monitor channel controls are located in the same numbered strips as the input channels.

Split:

> Means that the monitor channels are physically separate from the input channels and are probably located in the master section, to the right of the console.

Mute:

> Most studio mixers have Mute buttons on their input channels that turn off both the channel signal and any post-fade aux (effects send) sends. Pre-fade (foldback) sends are not normally affected.

PFL:

> PFL is short for Pre-Fade Listen, a system that allows any selected channel or Aux send/return return to be heard in isolation over the studio monitors. Because PFL is pre-fade (monitored prior to the channel fader), the level is independent of the channel fader position. When a channel's PFL button is pressed, all the other channels (on which the PFL has not been pressed) are excluded from the monitor mix and, at the same time, the signal level of the channel you are checking is displayed on one of the console's meters. PFL is generally used in this way to set up the individual channel input gain trims.

Solo:

> Isolates the channel in the monitor mix but, unlike PFL, the signal is post fader, which means that what you hear is the actual level of the signal in the mix. Most solo systems also retain the Pan position of the signal being checked which is why the term 'Solo In Place' or SIP is also commonly used. On a studio console, the main stereo output feeding the master stereo recorder, is not interrupted when PFL, Solo or SIP are used.

Aux Sends:

> Mixers invariably incorporate both pre-fade and post-fade aux sends. Aux sends provide a means to set up an independent mix of the channel signals, either for feeding effects or for providing a foldback mix. Pre-fade sends aren't affected by changes in the channel fader position which makes them ideal for setting up foldback mixes. Post-fade sends are derived after the channel fader, so if the channel fader is adjusted, the aux send level changes accordingly. This is necessary when adding effects such as echo or reverb because we normally want the relative levels of the dry signal and the effect to remain constant.

Insert Point:

> An insert point is simply a socket at which the signal flow may be interrupted allowing an external signal processor to be connected, for example a compressor or gate. Most consoles use TSR stereo jacks as insert points which means that a Y lead (stereo jack at one end, two mono jacks at the other) is needed to connect the external device. Alternatively, the insert points may be wired to a normalised patchbay. Insert points are usually provided in the Input channels, the Groups and at the main L/R stereo outputs.

Aux Returns:

> An aux return is, in effect, an additional line input channel but with fewer facilities than the main input channels. On smaller desks they will be permanently routed to the stereo mix buss while larger desks will provide the same routing arrangement as on the main input channels. Though these are included for use with effects, they can be used to add any line level signal (such as a tape machine, CD player or MIDI instrument) to the mix.

ALSO AVAILABLE FROM SANCTUARY TECHNIQUES

RECORDING AND PRODUCTION TECHNIQUES
by Paul White

ISBN 1 86074 188 6   £12.99/$14.95/Aus $29.95

This book takes a practical approach to demystifying the various techniques used to record and produce contemporary music. Aimed at the recording musician, the techniques described in this book are equally applicable to the home studio environment or the professional studio. The reader is taken through planning a recording session, getting the best performance from the artists and producing the best possible mix making creative use of effects and processors. The book concludes with a section on master tape formats and the processes involved in duplicating CDs, cassettes and vinyl records.

Clearly illustrated with comprehensive diagrams.

MIDI FOR THE TECHNOPHOBE
by Paul White

ISBN 1 86074 193 2   £11.95/$14.95/Aus $29.95

When Paul White first encountered MIDI, the main impediment to his progress was the very books claiming to explain it! Yet the basic principles of using MIDI to make and record music have direct counterparts in everyday life which we take for granted, such as television and the telephone. In this book the absolute beginner is introduced to the concept of MIDI by way of analogy with familiar technology. In just a few hours, with no confusing jargon, you'll find out how MIDI works, what hardware is needed to build your own system, and how to use that system to create, record and edit your own music.

Clearly illustrated with comprehensive diagrams.

MUSIC TECHNOLOGY – A SURVIVOR'S GUIDE
by Paul White

ISBN 1 86074 209 2   £11.95/$14.95/Aus $29.95

Written in Paul White's jargon-free, thoroughly comprehensive style, this book highlights common problems in recording and mixing music, addresses equipment dilemmas and does some troubleshooting. It discusses the debate on MIDI recording versus conventional multitracking, soundproofing, how to put together an accurate monitoring system, how to rescue an unsatisfactory mix and how to organise your studio for the best results. Most importantly it provides answers. Paul also provides an overview of equipment types and covers the hype and reality of vintage equipment.

Clearly illustrated with comprehensive diagrams.

HOT COUNTRY
by Lee Hodgson
ISBN 1 86074 138 X £19.99/$17.95/Aus $49.95

From James Burton to Albert Lee, Brent Mason and beyond, the real sound of country guitar is one of the most sought after among today's players. Whether you're a pro eager to add to your stylistic and technical abilities, or a newcomer who's drawn to that clean, twangy country sound, this book has something for everyone. Foreword by Albert Lee.

Includes one hour CD, full notation, chord boxes and tab.

RHYTHM
A STEP BY STEP GUIDE TO UNDERSTANDING RHYTHM FOR GUITAR
by David Mead
ISBN 1 86074 198 3 £19.99/$17.95/Aus $49.95

How does a guitarist develop a sense of rhythm? You can't learn it from a book…or can you? Imagine a book which lays out all you need to know to develop a razor sharp sense of timing with progressive exercises. One which even teaches you to read rhythmic notation painlessly and answers your tablature questions. This is that book.

Includes one hour CD, full notation, chord boxes and tab.

THE JAZZ STANDARD
by Frank Evans
ISBN 1 86074 163 0 £19.99/$19.95/Aus $49.95

The culmination of Frank Evans' forty years' performance and tutoring, *The Jazz Standard* contains more than twenty classic pieces by many of the greatest composers ever, from Richard Rodgers to Duke Ellington, George Gershwin to Cole Porter, all arranged for solo guitar with informative hints on playing technique.

Includes one hour CD, full notation and tab.

PHIL HILBORNE'S A-Z OF GREAT GUITAR RIFFS – VOLUMES I & II
by Phil Hilborne
ISBN 1 86074 153 3 (Vol I)/1 86074 207 6 (Vol II) £19.99/$19.95/Aus $49.95 (each volume)

The two books in this series form the most comprehensive collection yet of classic intros, rock riffs and signature guitar parts. From Aerosmith to Metallica in Volume I and Nirvana to ZZ Top in Volume II, *A-Z* is an invaluable encyclopaedia of great playing.

Includes one hour CD, full notation, chord boxes and tab.

For more information on titles from Sanctuary Publishing Ltd, please contact Sanctuary Publishing Ltd, 82 Bishops Bridge Road, London W6 2BB Tel: +44 (0) 171 243 0640 Fax: +44 (0) 171 243 0470. To order a title direct, please contact our distributors: (UK only) Macmillan Distribution Ltd Tel: 01256 302659. (US & Canada) Music Sales Corporation Tel: 1 800 431 7187. (Australia & New Zealand) Bookwise International Tel: 08268 8222.